Dimming of the Day
The Cricket Season of 1914

Simon Sweetman

Alas! Regardless of their doom,
The little victims play;
No sense have they of ills to come
Nor care beyond to-day
Yet see how all around 'em wait
The ministers of human fate
And black Misfortune's baleful train!
Ah, show them where in ambush stand,
To seize their prey, the murderous band!
Ah, tell them they are men!

Thomas Gray, Elegy written in a Country Churchyard

First published in Great Britain by
Association of Cricket Statisticians and Historians
Cardiff CF11 9XR.
© ACS, 2015

Simon Sweetman has asserted his right under the Copyright, Designs
and Patents Act 1988 to be identified as the author of this work.

British Library Cataloguing-in-Publication Data.
A catalogue record for this book is available from the British Library.

ISBN: 978 1 908 165 55 8
Typeset and printed by The City Press Leeds Ltd

Contents

Foreword

Eric Midwinter

SURREY DOING BADLY
German Army Lands in England

This was the text of a news vendor's placard in P.G.Wodehouse's satire *The Swoop! Or how Clarence saved England: a Tale of the Great Invasion*, published in 1909. Cricket and warfare are granted their true priorities in this spoof of the many pre-1914 tales of German invasion, most notable of them Erskine Childers' *The Riddle of the Sands* (1903). The contrast – some expecting war, some ridiculing the very notion – serves to demonstrate the ambiguities that beset the historian when looking at the opening phase of that dreadful conflict, the First World War. This ambivalence made itself manifest in several ways, all of which could marginally have affected the reactions of cricketers and cricket clubs to the crisis.

The counterpoint over the likelihood of war – and, indeed, whether the traditional foe of France might be the adversary – must be judged against the general background of a nation that had not experienced a major war since the long Revolutionary and Napoleonic struggles that had ended in 1815 with the Battle of Waterloo. And there had been no large-scale pitched battle on British soil since the Battle of Culloden in 1746. In the hundred years since the defeat of Napoleon, Britain had been involved in several often colonial conflicts, with the Crimean War of 1854/56 the nearest to home. With overwhelming naval authority – Britain had, in 1914, 27 large warships to Germany's 17 and France's ten – war was widely regarded as an away rather than as a home fixture. Moreover, because all the combatants looked on past warfare as the model, the set-piece battle was still *a la mode*. It is informative that when the coming war degenerated into a trench-based bloodbath, Kitchener complained that it wasn't war, rather like an old-fashioned buff moaning that the T20 version isn't cricket. Coloured clothing, another cricketing issue, touches on this subject: most 1914 armies were flamboyantly uniformed as for quick-fire martial array, one exception being the British dressed in the khaki they had turned to for action in South Africa.

Actually, the cricket time-span analogy was reversed, as the war turned out to be more a five-day Test than a one-day bash – and that is another factor. Very recent wars had been of relatively brief duration. The Franco-Prussian War of 1870/71 had been ten months: the First Boer War of 1880/81 had been less than five months; the Spanish-American War of 1898 had been less than five months, with only the Second Boer War of 1899/1902 at two years and seven months enduring substantially. Germany, for example, entered the First World War with only a six-month supply of gunpowder. Had it not been for the providential introduction of the new-fangled Haber-Bosch chemical process, the German army might have collapsed as early as 1916.

This kind of (chronological) backward thinking fuelled the idea that it 'would all be over by Christmas' or everyone would, as Kaiser Wilhem put it, "be home before the leaves have fallen from the trees." Here again there were shades of opinion, with some experts, including Kitchener himself, drawing perhaps on his experience of more spasmodic and attritional fighting against the Boers, believing that any new war might be prolonged. Others, such as H.G.Wells, were pessimistic about the scale of any coming warfare, although his 1908 dystopia *War in the Air* was basically thirty years too soon. What no single person anticipated was the type of war and the losses that would ensue. However, from a public viewpoint, all governments were keen to urge the brevity of war, should it come, as a booster for popular morale. The notion of a war that would be fought overseas as a pitched battle for a few months was, by and large, the expectation that one must understand in respect of the fag-end of the 1914 cricket season. This is the first factor in such an analysis.

The second component for those engaged in such a scrutiny is a further if slightly different kind of uncertainty between competing portraits of British life at that crucial time. The conventional picture is of an Edwardian idyll of lazy ease and rich grandeur, of enchanted sunlit days at country houses with gilded youth dispatching exquisite cover-drives across razored greenswards – this paradise to be irrevocably disturbed by the horror of war. That is not an idle depiction but there was another dimension to it, probably best summarised by George Dangerfield in his elegiac classic, *The Strange Death of Liberal England* (1935). Therein he captures another view of England in those months before the First World War, one of a state threatened by internal peril. He picks three strands of the increasing militancy of the Suffragette movement, the imminent risk of civil war in Ulster and the impending threat of a crippling general strike by a well-organised alliance of trades unions angered by the government apathy over poor living conditions. He and other historians see the trio loosely linked, as did some contemporaries, as portents of social revolution.

In fact some historians, notably Arno Mayer in, among other writings, his *Persistence of the Old Regime* (1971), argue that, in Britain as elsewhere, the war took the spotlight away from domestic strife, that ancient and modern trick of politicians anxious to dodge troubles at home with glories abroad. Whether by trick or by treat, the outbreak of war in 1914 certainly salvaged Britain from what some believe was its nearest modern approach to internal commotion of a tall order. What is important to realise, in looking how cricketers and other law-abiding citizens were disporting themselves during the cricket season of 1914, was that, for many, these more localised perils were much more compelling than an incident in faraway Sarajevo.

The possibility of war, then, was not the only, perhaps not the most pressing, question in most minds. Donald Read in *England 1868-1914*

(1979) as well as underlining the nation's proximity to social upheaval in 1914, writes of 'a widespread attitude' that it might all blow over, quoting especially young men, among them, Harold Macmillan, J.B.Priestley and – 'I was not emotionally aware of any close risk of catastrophe' – Hugh Dalton. As late as 27 July the *Manchester Guardian* wrote, 'the European war which has been talked about for so long that no one ever believed it would ever come'.

This links, by extension, with what Niall Ferguson in his very comprehensive and perceptive account *The Pity of War* (1998) terms 'the myth of war enthusiasm'. While never pretending there was not across Europe an energetic thrust for war, he again points to an equivocation. In converse to the jingoistic crowds that flocked through London following the announcement of war, there were, at all levels, grave doubts about the decision. When it came to volunteering, there was an initial reluctance more among the working than the middle classes. In the mainstream phase of volunteering up to February 1916 some 40% of those in the financial sector, commerce and the professions had joined up, compared with 28% of manual employees. Even taking into account the average better health of the former and the somewhat frail efforts to retain some of the latter in essential war industries, this is a massive divide. There were, of course, within these figures all kind of nuances; miners were over-represented and textile workers under-represented in volunteering and the Scots volunteered more readily than the English and the Irish less so.

How this might have played itself out in cricketing terms is a moot point, except to suggest that an aspect of the middle class eagerness to fight was clearly bound up with the public school ethos – 'the voice of the schoolboy rallies the ranks' – and its persistent affirmation of sport and duty. All but eight of the 539 boys who left Winchester between 1909 and 1915 volunteered, although hunting rather than cricket – 'a mounted....picnic in perfect weather' in Siegfried Sassoon's phrase – was the appropriate game: to men like Francis Grenfell, German soldiers were a species of fox or bear to be hunted for sport. Given the then preponderance of the middle classes in the cricketing fraternity, it might well be that cricket suffered as that 1914 summer wore on.

Those first two aspects – how war was perceived and how people judged its importance – are by way mainly of background canvas and characterisation. The third consideration is much more specific because it involves a closer scrutiny of the actual few weeks in question, namely the short period between the declaration of war on 4 August 1914 (but war was not declared against Austria-Hungary until 12 August) and the end of the cricket season. Here an almost diary-like finesse is required to trace the effects of war on cricket.

That very declaration was touch and go until the last hours. Asquith's Liberal cabinet was bitterly divided on the issue, with several members offering their resignations as late as 2 August and the government near collapse. Belgian neutrality was the official reason for the cabinet pulling back from the brink and, apart from John Morley and John Burns, showing solidarity, although the verdict of most historians is that they were, in practice, swayed by two other elements. First, there was the fear, strongly felt by Lloyd George, that the Germans would crush the French within weeks, as their army under the Prussian flag had done in 1870, with the consequence of them controlling the Channel coast. This was the Englishman's chief anxiety, scarcely helped by a similar belief among the myriad Parisians who were busily fleeing the city. Second, there was the fear that the rather more bellicose Conservative opposition would be only too delighted either to take over or form a war coalition.

Moreover, Winston Churchill, borrowing from the usual sign in the window of a fire damaged shop, called for 'business as usual', a dutiful injunction many obeyed, the general understanding being, in a nation untouched for centuries by serious alien incursion, that any war would be fought elsewhere and by the standing army. Until the last minute the ordinary hope was that somehow the problem would be solved and the pursuit of normal activity, inclusive perhaps of calmly playing cricket, might be a psychological token of this. The Foreign Secretary, Edward Grey, speaking in the House of Commons on 3 August, said, 'if we are engaged in war, we shall suffer it little more than we shall suffer if we stand aside.' According to A.J.P.Taylor, in his magisterial *English History 1914-1945* (1965) ministers assumed that "all would be over in a few months, if not a few weeks. The ordinary citizen would be little affected."

Next there were military vacillations about when to deploy the troops and how many of them should be utilised. Unlike the continental forces, the small British army, including the reservists who were promptly incorporated, was all-regular. Compared with Germany's 98.5 divisions comprising 2.2 million men, it consisted of but seven divisions, six infantry and one cavalry, 162,000 men in all, plus some 86,000 in reserve, that is following full-time service. In the distant background were 190,000, mainly Indian, colonial troops. Lord Haldane's nascent attempts to form a Territorial Army were in their early stages and only 7% of its members had undertaken to serve overseas. It was more akin to the militias and yeomanry of the past that had been recruited to deal with foreign assault or internal disorder. The continental armies, huge in size, were based on what later we would call national service, that is the build- up of vast forces by conscription for a period of training, each cohort then held in readiness for mobilisation. Some of this, especially in Russia, was low-level and sporadic, but it is in marked contrast to the British resistance, in spite of the pleading of Lord Roberts and others, to the introduction of obligatory military service. Some have seen the existence of quasi-martial youth organisations like the Boys Brigade and the Boy Scouts as a counter to this, while the officer cadet movement in the public schools was certainly destined to play its poignant part. Nonetheless, this essentially civil as opposed to martial focus is one that needs to be thoroughly understood while studying these early weeks of the war in Britain.

The British Expeditionary Force began to disembark at Boulogne, Le Havre and Rouen on 14 August and took up its position on the twenty mile length of the Mons-Conde Canal on 22 August to the left of their French allies, both armies poised to prevent the German advance into Belgium and France. It was here that the Schlieffen Plan, guaranteed to finish hostilities within six weeks, would be tested – and found wanting. There had been what the military historian, John Keegan, in his *The First World War* (1998) described as 'a curious interval of calm', almost three weeks of inactivity following the onset of war. This inaction was unusual and, from a purely English viewpoint, a further reinforcement of domestic composure or, more specifically, three cricketing weekends.

There followed a grim irony. For about the last time in this or any other future war, there was a straightforward old-style gun battle which the British won hands down. This was the First Battle of Mons. Outnumbered by six divisions to four the BEF, which Kaiser scornfully dismissed as 'a contemptible little army,' destroyed the German opposition. With most of them hard-bitten veterans of the South African War and with extra pay having motivated them to achieve a grade of marksmanship, they ensconced themselves in the industrial properties around the canal and utilised their superior Lee-Enfield rifles to lethal effect. So damaging were their 'fifteen rounds a minute' salvoes that the dismayed German troops thought that they were suffering from extensive machine-gun fire. To extend the parallel, the battle lasted about as long as the Battle of Waterloo, about the same number of British soldiery, some 30,000, were involved and the losses comparatively mild by later yardsticks – 1,500 dead, 6,500 injured, but also the same as in the 1815 victory.

I should declare an interest. My favourite Great Uncle Sam, having been at the Relief of Ladysmith in the Boer War, was one of these genuine 'Old Contemptibles', who won the Military Medal, happily recovered his sight after mustard gas blinding and later distinguished himself in the civil defence on Manchester Docks during the blitz in the Second World War. So filial pride as well as patriotism may slew the judgement that had the French acquitted themselves with the same competence as Uncle Sam and his mates to the British right at the Battle of the Sambre, the war might have taken a distinctly different and maybe shorter course.

The immediate point, however, is to note that the first news item of the war, from a British standpoint, reflected the conventional view that warfare was conducted by a standing army which fought pitched battles and that we were very good at it. The press, always encouraged to be optimistic, cheerfully reported this success. No cause for panic, then, for yet a few more days of the cricket season.

It was only at this point that things began to unravel. The French defeat on the Sambre led to 'the Great Retreat' that also forced the victorious BEF to retire, the Germans sustained their advance through Belgium, there was ferocious fighting on and around the Marne and both sides undertook 'the Race to the Sea', as each desperately tried to avoid being outflanked. That was the key to this novel form of industrial war, with trenches strung out from the North Sea coast through eastern France to the Swiss border. Mass mobilisation, heavy manufacturing back-up and the fast rail transport of men and supplies were the chief accessories of the coming years long and bloody stalemate.

By now it was well into September with the cricket season moving into the shadows. Slowly the sobering penny was beginning to drop. Much was made in the newspapers of the atrocities committed by the German army against the civilian population of Belgium. Unhappily, there was not much need for hyperbole. Belgian refugees were by now flooding into Britain. Suddenly the casualty lists began to lengthen ominously. By the end of the month half the BEF had been killed or wounded. The Fall of Antwerp on 10 October and the first Battle of Ypres (20 October to 22 November) – note the length of time that first-ever 'trench' battle took – were the first indicators that every prediction about the style and most predictions about the duration of the war had been proved false.

One can trace the growing realisation of this tragic outcome back in Britain. *The Sportsman* of 27 August carried just about W.G.Grace's only intervention in political affairs, with his letter calling on 'all first-class cricketers of suitable age' to enlist and for county cricket to be halted 'for it is not fitting that at a time like the present that able-bodied men should play day after day and pleasure-seekers look on.' Simon Rae, Grace's most complete and thoughtful biographer, does comment that a further round of the county championship was played despite its publication and, of course, the letter was directed at first-class spectator cricket not club cricket.

Lord Roberts made a stirring speech which included a reference to 'people who went on playing cricket at this time', while Archie MacLaren used the pages of *The World of Cricket*, the magazine he professed to edit, to describe Kaiser Wilhelm as 'that hog in armour' and 'that crowned madman'. Nonetheless, the descent into what Benny Green described as 'hysterical idiocy' did take some time to occur. For example, it was October before MacLaren enlisted as a lieutenant in the Army Service Corps and, usually in company with Captain G.L.Jessop, engaged in a three-year stint as a recruiting officer. It was only at the end of August that Kitchener persuaded the cabinet, still very much opposed to compulsion, that he must raise a 'New Army' of seventy divisions, a huge advance on the basic seven that formed the BEF. This was the start of the 'Kitchener wants You' campaign. It was remarkably successful. He asked for an initial 200,000 – the first week in September alone attracted 115,000; the figure was 750,000 by the end of that month, and the spate of recruits continued at an average of 125,000 per month until the June of 1915: 2.5 million men had volunteered by March 1916 when conscription had finally to be introduced, which is extremely impressive; it was 25% of those eligible.

That does, of course, mean that 75% did not volunteer whereas there is a vague legendary belief that every young man rushed to the colours. But it is still a massive army of purely volunteers. It is true that there were social pressures – the financial turmoil increased the rate of unemployment abruptly, the recruitment techniques were wondrously productive; female and peer-group pressure was intense, whilst as at every juncture since the

Crusades there was sheer impulse.

Nonetheless, in practical effect, there was no substantial volunteering before the end of August, very close to the end of the cricket season.

In looking at the effect on recreational cricket as the summer of 1914 slowly gave way to the autumn, one has to blinker the eyes to hindsight. We all now know what a tragically gory and largely senseless exercise the First World War was. Those living at the time when war broke out did not. They expected that, if war came, it would be in A.J.P.Taylor's words 'an act of state..... With which ordinary citizens had little to do.' They were in for one of the most terrible collective shocks ever inflicted on the British people; ordinary citizens had much to do in that the war came to affect every home in many ways. It took a month, maybe two or three months, fully to understand the significance of this sea-change and those few weeks coincided with the end of the cricket season.

It was to be a traumatic experience, so much so that I have advanced the hypothesis elsewhere that, for entirely negative reasons, the First World War is probably the most salient event in the history of English cricket.

Yet, for those first few weeks in August, no one quite understood what was about to occur and that may well have affected, one way or another, the fate of local club cricket.

Eric Midwinter

Chapter One

The Structure of Cricket in 1914

The cricketing world of 1914 was rather different from the one to which we are accustomed.

The Imperial Cricket Conference had been formed in 1909 and had three members. England and Australia's matches had now been brought under the auspices of MCC and the Australian Board of Control which had just won its bitter struggle with the players. England and Australia met regularly. South Africa were also a Test side, though their performances in the Triangular Tournament of 1912 suggested that they were not really a match for the others at full strength.

The ICC had organised a programme of tours. Australia would go to South Africa in 1914/15, England would go to Australia in 1915/16 and Australia would come to England in 1916 with South Africa following in 1917. It is notable that there would be no Test matches in England between 1912 and 1916.

In addition there were private tours arranged from various parts of the Empire (and from the USA). In 1911, for instance, there were tours from Germantown (in Philadelphia) and by an Indian team captained by the Maharajah of Patiala and including the 'untouchable' slow left-arm bowler Palwankar Baloo: this team played first-class matches, though with no definition in place, that was a matter of what fixtures one could arrange. In 1914 there were tours by Merion (from Pennsylvania) and by a team from Egypt and the Sudan. Neither of these teams was first-class, playing against club sides. These were also strictly gentlemanly affairs, the members of the team paying for themselves.

The first-class game consisted of the County Championship, Oxford and Cambridge Universities, some scratch games at the end of season festivals, various MCC fixtures, the Free Foresters' matches against the Universities and the showcase matches of which Gentlemen v Players was the most significant. In fact there were three such games arranged for 1914. The Lord's game was the one that mattered, but the Oval match was of little less significance: the one at Scarborough at the end of the season would be little more than a romp.

The County Championship had expanded to 16 teams in 1905, but most of them were essentially cannon fodder. Since 1890 and the start of the "official" list of champions, there had only been seven different champions and of these Middlesex, Nottinghamshire and Warwickshire had only claimed one each. Surrey, Yorkshire, Kent and Lancashire were dominant (and indeed there was to be no new name added to the list of champions until Derbyshire won in 1936). It was not a league in the true sense as counties arranged their own matches within certain parameters (such as playing nobody more than twice) and did not all play the same number of games, meaning that an averaging system was needed. Some, though not all, of the traditional Bank Holiday fixtures were already in place.

The University sides were strong, especially in batting. There was a seamless route from the "great" public schools to Oxford and Cambridge and then to a county captaincy or at least a few years of cricket before turning to a career. All the three-day games played by the University sides were regarded as first-class (and were given that sort of treatment by the press); these included matches against various people's XIs. The Army v The Navy and Ireland v Scotland would also be included.

The Minor Counties Championship (the second-class counties) had existed since 1895 when the dividing line between first-class and second-class cricket was drawn. Like the first-class game minor county cricket was organised by clubs whose members were the gentlemen of the county. The Minor Counties, like the weaker first-class counties, depended on the amateurs being available to turn out and for some of the wealthier members regularly to put their hands in their pockets. The best minor county sides (Staffordshire or Durham, for instance) were probably as strong as the weaker first-class counties.

Qualification rules depending on birthplace or residence had been introduced for the County Championship in 1873 and were strictly enforced for the professionals. Amateurs were allowed more latitude and there are many cases where the basis for qualification is difficult to see. With very few exceptions, professionals stayed where they had started, often for twenty years or more.

Below the county game was a layer of clubs, some of long standing, who played only friendly matches. This was true especially in the south of England though they existed throughout Britain. These were effectively gentlemen's clubs though they might employ professionals who would be groundsmen, coaches and net bowlers. This was even more true of the wandering XIs – I Zingari, Eton Ramblers, Band of Brothers, Incogniti and the rest, whose membership was carefully restricted to gentlemen who had been to a public school and usually Oxbridge.

These games were noticed. *The Observer* regularly featured a long run-down on Saturday's club cricket in the London region, with the fixtures for next week and a long piece on notable performances, then summarised (one-line) scores. The magazine *Cricket* had published the results of club matches (mostly in the London area), and had in fact charged the clubs for their insertion. By 1914, though, the magazine was in its short-lived variant as *World of Cricket* and no longer included club scores.

Most cricket in England, Scotland and Wales, however, was played in leagues. In the north and midlands and in Scotland (where there was a one-day county championship) league cricket was the dominant format. Clubs in the larger leagues (Lancashire, Bradford or North Staffs) were organised very much like the football clubs of the day, dominated by the mercantile middle class, rather than the gentry and professional classes. Even by this time the bigger league clubs could lure players away from county cricket to a more reliable source of income with a season's contract and the certainty of playing every week. Sydney Barnes was the classic example but there were many others. One very significant difference was that league clubs might well make payments to amateurs as talent money or expenses: that would have been totally out of the question for 'club' sides.

There were leagues at many levels. *The Manchester Guardian* published fixtures for the Manchester and District Association, Lancashire League, Central Lancashire League, South Lancashire League, Manchester Federation, Manchester League, Bolton League and "miscellaneous" which was the club rather than the league circuit. The clubs playing to the southern "amateur" ethos tended to be located in the leafier areas with Cheshire well represented. In particular the Manchester Club played at Old Trafford and many county amateurs would turn out for it.

The *Manchester Guardian* of 27 July saw substantial reports on Lancashire League games – Cecil Parkin (about to make his Lancashire debut) took 7 – 44 against Burnley. The paper also looked at the South Lancs League and the Yorkshire Council.

On 30 July Longsight had beaten Manchester under the heading M&D Association. The 31 July results in full include Shropshire Gentlemen v Free Foresters and the first match of the Shavington Festival at Market Drayton between Captain Lonsdale's XI and Liverpool Athenians.

On 31 July fixtures include M&D Association, Lancashire League, Central Lancashire League, South Lancashire League, Manchester League, Bolton League, High Peak League, Manchester Federation (and a hefty list of miscellaneous matches).

Full scores are given as late as 27 August for Manchester and District Association, and reduced scores for M&D Federation, where Manchester Press played South-West Manchester at Old Trafford. In the middle of the county scores was Old Rossallians against Malton Club and Ground.

The *Sports Argus* in Birmingham reported Birmingham League games, suburban league games and friendly matches. It reported too on the final of the Aston Schools Trophy, where Gower Street had beaten Canterbury Road. There were league tables too from the Birmingham Works League and the Parks Association which ran to eight divisions: not to mention the Kidderminster League, the Prudential League and the Wesleyan League. The final of the Dudley Works knock-out was played at Palethorpe's and Netherton Ironworks at the County Ground before a crowd of about 1,000.

Throughout the country, however, leagues were the rule rather than the exception at a level below that of the best clubs. They existed for villages, for works teams, for elementary schools and for the Sunday Schools. Large factories ran internal leagues. To take just one example the *Grantham*

Journal reported on teams such as Kesteven Asylum and the Belvoir Hunt Servants playing in the local leagues.

The *Express* carried fixtures and scores for the South London League, the Harrow and Wealdstone League and the Battersea Churches Association games on Wandsworth Common. There were small local leagues running in Kent, Sussex, Suffolk and Norfolk. In Cornwall, Wales and Scotland league cricket dominated as it did in the North and Midlands.

In the south of England the leagues were later to wither away in the face of the scorn of the Club Cricket Conference, founded during the war to help arrange friendly matches, but later to crusade against league cricket.

There is an interesting quote from the website of the Club Cricket Conference no less (based on research by Duncan Stone),

> The CCC was founded in 1915 to help clubs cope with fixtures during the Great War, but the organisation lost its way in the 1950s and 1960s. This was a dark period when the CCC could justifiably be regarded as reactionary and even destructive while aspirations of so many club cricketers were beginning to change. In the post-War era a rule in the CCC's original constitution was used to block all attempts to introduce competition and coaching in the south. That sort of behaviour is completely disowned by the CCC nowadays.

The CCC's original rule read, 'It shall be an indispensible condition that this London Club Cricket Conference shall neither recognise, approve of, nor promote any cup or league system.' 'London' might be significant.

In fact the summary for Duncan Stone's paper reads,

> As the late Victorian and Edwardian upper classes' power declined, some of the sporting elites were determined to maintain their social and cultural hegemony. Within amateur cricket, this was to be maintained by the Club Cricket Conference (CCC), the aims of which were to 'control and safeguard amateur cricket along strictly non-competitive lines'. Although largely reactionary, the CCC, due in no small part to its social origins, exerted a disproportionate influence over amateur club cricket in the South of England – especially with regard to the aggressive suppression of leagues. Although the historiography suggests that the CCC were very successful in this endeavour, leagues and cups existed throughout the South from the early 1880s. The historical oversight of what became a predominantly working-class mode of cricket, and the game's cultural meaning, reflects the social origins and influence of the CCC's elite founders (and many historians) over the game and its image.

Far more attention was paid by the press to cricket at the public schools, especially the "great " schools who played their traditional rivals at Lord's. Cricket was a major activity at these schools and they would run second and junior elevens as well as "the Eleven". They would play other schools, but would also play local and wandering clubs as well as MCC. In 1914 Hurstpierpoint College, then a school of 186 boys, ran three teams and played a total of 25 matches. *The Times* published school scores and wrote long commentaries, but other newspapers produced full scores as well. Many pages of *Wisden* were devoted to their performances. *The Times* feels as if its cricket pages were written by and for a small coterie of the upper classes looking for the scores of the younger generation.

The other scores for the London Press would be those of various military teams (the Household Brigade seemed to spend most of its time playing cricket) and public school Old Boys' sides.

Then, of course, there was country house cricket, nostalgically presented as the game where the upper classes and their social inferiors mixed. Even now it may be impossible to rescue recreational cricket – country house and village – from that golden haze. They were the days when the visiting team still arrived for matches in a two-horse brake (uncomfortable but romantic as described by Siegfried Sassoon). His chapter *The Flower Show Match* (there may be an indication here that the toffs did not join the village team every week) and Hugh de Selincourt's *The Cricket Match* (published in 1924) look back. If the cricket match in *England, their England* is set in the early twenties, it harks back to the traditional model (one could, of course, follow the account all the way back to Mary Mitford).

What Flora Thompson (writing from the lower strata), however, said in *Lark Rise to Candleford* suggests that this might not have been entirely true,

> A few of the young men played cricket in the summer. One young man was considered a good bowler locally and he would sometimes get up a team to play one of the neighbouring villages. This once led to a curious little conversation on his doorstep. A lady had alighted from her carriage to ask, or rather, command him to get up a team to play "the young men", meaning her sons on holiday from school, and a few of their friends. Naturally, Frank wanted to know the strength of the team he was to be up against." You'd want me to bring a good team, I suppose, ma'am, he asked respectfully. "Well, yes," said the lady. "The young gentlemen would enjoy a good game. But don't bring too good a team. They wouldn't want to be beaten."

> "That's what she calls cricket," said Frank, grinning broadly at her retreating figure.

There was no organised women's cricket at this time. There had been efforts in the past to manufacture a commercial product, but by this time women who might have played at school if they had been expensively educated tended to play odd games as part of village celebrations or against the gentlemen of the club playing left-handed or with broomsticks.

Far more than now, both men and boys played some sort of cricket at a time when it shared the year with football so that it was perfectly possible to play both at any level.

Chapter Two

The Making of the Myth of a Golden Age

Before we look at what happened, perhaps we should turn to what was lost, as traditional accounts have seen it as the time when cricket was most truly cricket. Golden Ages, by definition, are in the past, and they represent something from which we have fallen away. Plato, basing himself on Hesiod, saw it that way, setting off all kinds of attempts to find the lost city of Atlantis by people who could not tell fact from fiction: the myth of the Garden of Eden is another of the same sort.

There is a general myth about the years before the Great War. George Dangerfield, having more or less decisively demolished the myth of pre-war tranquillity (before Downton Abbey and its like brought it back) put it well in 1935

> Standing beside Rupert Brooke's moonlit grave, one looks back. All the violence of the pre-war world has vanished, and in its place there glow, year into backward year, the diminishing vistas of that other England, the England where the Grantchester church clock stood at ten to three, where there was Beauty, Certainty and Quiet, and where nothing was real. Today we know it for what it was: but there are moments, very human moments, when we could almost find it in our hearts to envy those who saw it, and never lived to see the new world.[1]

Looking back from even further away, we have the added obstruction to our vision of the Second World War and the natural tendency to reflect the values of that war back to the First.

Cricketers are terribly prone to this worship of the past. Whether it was John Nyren in *The Cricketers of My Time* or James Pycroft in *The Cricket Field* in 1851 bemoaning the way the game had gone downhill, or any of a swathe of writers complaining that no wicketkeepers in the 1950s stood up to fast bowling any more, or today's commentators wondering where the fast bowlers have gone, yesterday always looks better.

Surely, though, the golden age of cricket deserves its name? The age of Ranji and Fry, of MacLaren and Jessop, of the late Indian summer of WG?

The Edwardian age – in cricket as well as in popular imagining of the past - acquired its gilt finish because of what came after it. Writing in *History of Cricket* (published in 1926) H.S. Altham subscribes strongly to the myth and all its fictional appearances are the same (look at L.P.Hartley in *The Go-Between*, even though it was not published until 1953). In these accounts the sun shines and nobody sits morosely in the pavilion (except

---

1   George Dangerfield, *The Strange Death of Liberal England*, 1935

for 1902 when the wet summer merely made Victor Trumper's batting seem even more extraordinary).

The myth still has power: if we look at *Half of the Human Race*[2], published in 2011, the romance between the cricketer and the suffragette does little to suggest that others besides women might be suffering. As so often, the working class are invisible except as domestic servants.

After 1918, there were those who had survived; Pelham Warner for instance and, of course, Neville Cardus with his reminiscences of MacLaren and Spooner and of early visits to Old Trafford did much to stoke the furnace. It is hardly a surprise for those surviving the Great War that the years before it took on a particular glow. Especially was this true for the upper and upper middle classes who felt a loss of status with the rise of organised labour, but mainly felt the terrible loss of life of a generation who died in Flanders and elsewhere.

After the war, the landowning class – very important for a certain type of cricket, and that the most gilded of all – suffered from the loss of rents with the agricultural depression, and some of them for the loss of their investments. Of course, they blamed it all on increased taxes. The years before 1914 seemed all the more carefree.

Altham in fact referred to the golden age of batting (and headed his chapter so), though his contention was that the bowling was strong as well, serving to enhance the glow of the batsmanship. Cardus in his *English Cricket*[3] said the same thing – it was the golden age of batsmanship – and that was based on the gilded batting of the great amateur batsmen. Cardus went on to identify it as a golden age *per se* because there were good bowlers about and because Australians looked on it as such (largely, but not entirely, because of Victor Trumper). Cardus's book was written before the Second World War was over and when he was in Australia and not expecting to write on cricket again and so a certain sentimental nostalgia may have crept in.

Any golden age of amateur batting was over well before 1914. In 1902 England's batting at Birmingham had included Fry, Ranjitsinjhi, MacLaren, Jackson and Jessop. In 1914 the leading amateur batsmen (by average) were Sydney Smith of Northants and Donald Knight of Surrey.

Lawrence Booth said, talking about Tom Maynard,

> Sportsmen are not supposed to die young. They may lapse into premature decline once their careers are over; they may be taken from us too soon by injury. But to die young is the preserve of the rock star. It is not part of the sporting deal, with its athleticism and gilded youth.[4]

There is a different flavour to this than to Victorian cricket in general. The backlash against the starchy Victorian rectitude which was now seen

---

2   Anthony Quinn, *Half of the Human Race*, 2011
3   Neville Cardus, *English Cricket* Collins, 1945
4   Lawrence Booth, *TopSpin*, email 19 June 2012

as hypocrisy, (Lytton Strachey's *Eminent Victorians* was published in 1918), was beginning and perhaps people were less likely to see cricket as providing moral lessons (a hard stance to maintain when your superstar was W.G.Grace) and more to see it as entertainment, both to play and watch. If, however, it had been the best game because it did you good, it was now to be the best game, well, because it was the best game to watch or play.

Some at least of the writing before the war was already tinged with nostalgia, suggesting that the perfection of the wickets (all that Nottingham marl) now meant that mediocre batsmen could survive unreasonably. Ranji's *Jubilee Book of Cricket* (1897) but more so Pelham Warner's *Imperial Cricket* helped to feed the myth. The website *Sportspages* calls it,

> A monumental volume charting the rise and development of the game in every country of the Empire including such far-flung outposts as Bermuda, Egypt, and the Sudan, Fiji, Solomon Islands and Hong Kong. Also chapters on "Cricket and the royal family", Oxford and Cambridge cricket, I Zingari, Free Foresters. Contributors include F.S.Ashley-Cooper, A.C.M.Croome, Andrew Lang, Cecil Headlam and S.P.Foenander.

It came out originally in 1912, the year of the Triangular Tournament which was the first thing to be arranged following the formation of the ICC – itself a profoundly political act.

What have cricket's later historians made of the Edwardian age?

Peter Wynne-Thomas[5] heads his chapter *The Golden Age?* and points out that the upper middle class had hijacked cricket at the highest level. The sport was drifting away from the lower strata of society and the magnet of the soccer field was attracting the workers.

Sir John Major, whose book[6] ends with 1914, says as cricket enjoyed its greatest days, the clock was winding down to war.

Rowland Bowen[7] calls his chapter The Golden Age of Cricket 1894 – 1914 and says there is one major argument in favour of so considering the twenty years before the First World War that it was, or seemed then, or sometimes seems now, to have been a "Golden Age" in so very many other things. Bowen also remarks – percipiently – that in fifty years all this may look very different.

County clubs were not professional organisations. They were and continued to be (most of them to this day) members' clubs, run for the benefit of members – not for the players or paying spectators - who helped to keep them afloat. They employed professionals originally to play with the members and to bowl to them in the nets, then to bolster the county side, but if there was a member wanting to play, then at most counties he would have priority and a professional would have to make way. For

5   Peter Wynne-Thomas, *The History of Cricket*, HMSO, 1997
6   John Major, *More than a Game*, HarperCollins, 2007
7   Rowland Bowen, *Cricket: A History*, Eyre & Spottiswoode, 1970

the poorer counties, if there was a shortfall at the end of the year, there might be an aristocratic patron who would put his hand in his pocket. When Hampshire played at Bournemouth there would be theatrical performances put on in aid of the county's funds. And the poorer counties could still only afford to employ a few professionals in any case and those would be bowlers because bowlers could service the members in the nets. Local town clubs were run on the same model.

Altham and Swanton's *A History of Cricket* [8] which was published in 1938, having originally been written by H.S.Altham as a series of articles in *The Cricketer* and published in book form in 1926, simply does not mention the war, moving from chapters ending in 1914 to those beginning in 1919 or 1920. Not even the loss of life among public schools cricketers was mentioned. Perhaps it was too raw a subject for the history of the game, although when the two volume edition appeared in 1962 Swanton began the second volume with a brief chapter entitled Counting the Cost.

Eric Parker, writing *The History of Cricket* for the Lonsdale Library [9] (undated but from internal evidence 1949) does refer to the war, but the way the book is written it is not so much a general history as split into sections on counties, Eton v Harrow, and so on. An earlier edition had contained pieces from various cricketers and was entitled *The Game of Cricket*. Parker had written a biography of H.V.Hesketh Prichard which included his experiences in the trenches, so knew something about the reality of war.

However, in referring to the 1914 Eton v Harrow match he wrote

> England was at war with the enemy of all that the schools of England stand for. E.W.Hornung, in a poem, "Lord's Leave 1915", has told something of what lies beyond the turnstiles of St.John's Wood. Two stanzas out of nine hold the same meaning today as when they were written thirty years ago
>
> > Cricket? 'Tis Sanskrit to the super-Hun
> > Cheap cross between Caligula and Cassius
> > To whom speech, prayer and warfare are all one
> > Equally gaseous!
> >
> > Playing a game's beyond him and his hordes:
> > Theirs but to play the snake or wolf or vulture:
> > Better one sporting lesson learnt at Lord's
> > Than all their Kultur

Hornung was writing shortly after the Second World War, but it still reads very harshly. Hornung mentions that R.St.L.Fowler and the Hon J.N.Manners of Eton died in the war, but it is not part of his history to discuss 1914.

If we turn again to the iconoclastic Major Rowland Bowen [10], writing in

---

8   H.S.Altham & E.W.Swanton, *A History of Cricket*, George Allen & Unwin, 1938
9   Eric Parker, *The History of Cricket*, Lonsdale Library, Vol XXX,
10   Rowland Bowen ibid

1970, he devotes a chapter to the First World War and his first paragraph is worth repeating

> In a curiously subconscious way, those who lived before and took part in the First World War seem to have been aware that great, indeed enormous changes would result from that war, in all sorts of ways they could hardly guess. Indeed the full working out of those changes would not come until the Second World War, partly because the awareness had been subconscious rather than overt. This is, of course, why it is those who came to mature thought after the last war are unable to grasp what the general social set-up was before it, whereas those who came to mature thought after the First World War can very well understand the pre-1914 period. Both, to the present generation, are now history; but to the generation of thirty or forty years ago, not even the first seemed to be history. Yet there seems to have been this subconscious awareness of something enormous happening. It can be seen in the way that cricket came to a halt in August 1914 for all but a very few games – not only county cricket but club cricket too[11]. It can be seen, in its darker side, in the utterly fantastic war hysteria which gripped responsible citizens.

Benny Green wrote *A History of Cricket* in 1988[12] (carefully calling it "A" rather than "The" history). Talking of W.G., he quoted Conan Doyle as testifying that the cause of the Doctor's death was a broken heart in the face of appalling slaughter of a war whose methods he could not comprehend, and whose mindless brutality destroyed his faith in his own species.

Green has a chapter headed *Casualty Lists*, and talks about the slightly strange way that county cricket went on after the declaration of war simply because there was no machinery to stop it.

Peter Wynne-Thomas's *The History of Cricket: from the Weald to the World*[13] quotes an editorial from the 8 August edition of A.C.MacLaren's magazine *The World of Cricket* (shortly to collapse under its debts, like most of MacLaren's business ventures).

> Armageddon may well be at hand. As one writes the talk is all of War-War-War! Cricket is naturally pushed into the background – naturally and rightly – big a part as the greatest of games plays in our natural life. Yet when the thrilling call – who is on our side? – goes forth, the debt the nation owes to cricket ought not to be forgotten. In spite of the occasional squabbles – Sydney barracking, Bloemfontein incidents, and the like – cricket has perhaps done more than anything else to weld together in links of sympathy the Mother Country and her widespread children.

Wynne-Thomas mentions that some of the players were recalled to their

---

11   Up to a point.
12   Benny Green, *A History of Cricket*, Barrie & Jenkins, 1988
13   Peter Wynne-Thomas, *The History of Cricket: from the Weald to the World*, Stationery Office, 1997

regiments, and suggests that the words of W.G.Grace (and then Lord Roberts) brought things to a stop.

John Major's *More Than a Game*[14] which describes itself as the history of cricket's early years, ends in 1914. He says,

> The war that would be "over by Christmas" was greeted with enthusiasm. Young men rushed to enlist before it was over. They need not have hurried. A generation died, and cricket was not exempt.

Finally there is Eric Midwinter, whose *The Cricketer's Progress: Meadowland to Mumbai*[15] is dated 2010. Professor Midwinter's thesis is that the war threw cricket into a stasis from which it has never recovered, and he says,

> The First World War is possibly the most significant episode in the history of cricket. The 1914-18 war abruptly stopped cricket in its tracks. It was cricket's equivalent of the Fall of the Roman Empire, the collapse of a great institution, but one still able to cast influential shadows.

He also mentions that in 1914 'net practice was stopped at the Oval because the players were being jeered at by men off the tram cars as they rattled by the ground.'

So there are some doubts about the rosy glow of the pre-war world: but what was it really like for those who were living and working through it?

---

14   John Major, *More Than A Game*, Harper Perennial, 2008
15   Eric Midwinter, *The Cricketer's Progress: Meadowland to Mumbai*, Third Age Press, 2010

Chapter Three
The Picture of Britain

The funeral of Edward VII in May 1910 was probably the grandest imperial spectacle that Britain had ever seen. Among the mourners were nine kings, five heirs apparent, forty imperial or royal highnesses, seven queens (four dowagers and three regnant)[16] and a host of royal hangers-on. Edward had been known as "the uncle of Europe" and as far as crowned heads were concerned this was an entirely literal description as Victoria's progeny spread across the continent. Surely so grand a spectacle, so much bling, must indicate a country and a world at peace with itself.

But security had to be high. The police would have worried about anarchists, suffragettes, militant workers and various Irish groups, all of whom had their grievances.

So what might be called the Julian Fellowes view of the Edwardian age as a time of peace and prosperity, of untroubled games of cricket watched by large crowds who had come to see the great amateur batsmen of the age, is not quite how it was. Neither the nation nor the cricket field was quite so serene.

The nation was certainly not undivided. George Sherston's aunt in *Memoirs of a Fox-hunting Man*[17] worked by a social code which divided the world into people on whom one could call and people who were socially impossible. Those who were socially impossible have become to a great extent historically invisible.

Harold Laski said it more strongly,

> The Edwardian poor have attracted little attention in imaginative literature and play almost no part in commonly held images of Edwardian England. But to look at the domestic lives of the poor, both urban and rural, is to shadow our picture of upper- and middle-class life with horror and dismay.

A sign of the tension was the constitutional crisis that had developed over Lloyd George's 1909 Budget. The permanent Tory majority in the House of Lords rejected the Finance Bill (with breath-taking arrogance for a party reduced to a rump in the House of Commons). It was passed – reluctantly – but the consequence was the 1911 Parliament Act which constrained the powers of the House of Lords who could now delay legislation passed in the Commons but could not ultimately prevent its passage and could not stop money bills at all. That defeat had come about only after the new king

---

16   Barbara Tuchman, *The Guns of August*, 1963
17   Siegfried Sassoon, *Memoirs of a Fox-hunting man*

– George V – agreed reluctantly that if necessary he would create 500 new peers to swamp the Tory majority.

A list found in Asquith's papers was published in his biography (by J.A.Spender and Cyril Asquith in 1932) and (unromantically) is not full of cricketers, though it is not a complete list. Lionel King, writing in *The Cricket Statistician*[18], claimed that Asquith's grandson, Mark Bonham Carter, had suggested in a conversation with him that the full (original) list included W.G.Grace, C.B.Fry, Sir Arthur Conan Doyle and even Ranjitsinjhi: this list too, it was said, was found in Asquith's papers.

But the Tory party, still believing in its divine right to run the country, was not finished and was to inflame the next crisis. The most serious potential disturbance of that Edwardian peace was the threat of civil war in Ulster.

The third Irish Home Rule Bill was introduced into Parliament in April 1911. Gladstone's two earlier attempts had failed, but after 1910 the Liberal majority in the House of Commons had fallen sharply, and Asquith as Prime Minister needed the votes of the Irish Nationalists. It would have given Home Rule to the whole of Ireland, and was bitterly resented by the Protestant majority in the six counties of Ulster. There were two elections in 1910 and Irish Home Rule was a dominant question in both.

By 28 September 1912 half a million people in the North had signed the Ulster Covenant, described as a pledge to defend themselves against the prospect of Home Rule. Both sides – the Ulster Volunteers and the Irish National Volunteers – were arming themselves with smuggled weapons. The Act was due to become law in 1914 and (as we shall see) the threat of civil war in Ireland seemed a good deal more significant than the prospect of European war even days before the outbreak of that war. There was much running about trying to reach a compromise, but the Ulster Protestants wanted no compromise, and there was a growing militancy in the Catholic South. In March 1914 the mutiny at the Curragh showed that – when it came to the Ulster Protestants – the government could not rely on the Army.

Then there were the "suffragettes" as the *Daily Mail* sneeringly called them. *The Times*, more polite, always said "suffragists". The Women's Social and Political Union, devoted to direct action, did not stop at breaking shop windows and during the spring and summer of 1913 had turned to arson. At least two cricket pavilions were burned (they would be unguarded and there was little risk to life). Hotels, railway stations, racecourse grandstands and golf clubhouses were also targets. In a six-month period in 1913 there were apparently some 250 arson attacks.

The Edwardian era was certainly not a "golden age" for most workers, as those who have read Robert Tressell's *The Ragged Trousered Philanthropists* will know. The Taff Vale judgement of the House of Lords in 1901 allowed employers to sue unions for losses incurred through strike action. This was reversed by the Trades Disputes Act of 1906, with

---

18   *The Cricket Statistician* , No.163, Autumn 2013

the Liberal government supported after the 1906 election by a much increased Labour representation. There were 872 strikes in 1911, including major strikes in the docks and the railways. 1 March 1912 saw the first national miners' strike: *The Times* called it 'the greatest catastrophe that has threatened the country since the Spanish Armada.' This resulted not in revolution but in an Act which established a minimum wage in the industry though the quantum was to be decided locally.

Problems were not over. The period from 1910 to 1914 is sometimes known as "the great unrest" and the more excitable saw socialist revolution on the way. In his memoirs David Lloyd George said that in 1914,

> Trouble was threatening in the railways, mining, engineering and building industries, disagreements were active not only between employers and employed, but in the internal organisation of the workers.

A strong 'rank and file' movement, keenly critical of the policies and methods of the official leaders of trade unionism had sprung up and was gaining steadily in strength.

Such was the state of the home front when the nation plunged into war.

And as the Siege of Sydney Street in 1911, and varied lurid fictional accounts suggested, where other folk devils failed there were always the Anarchists!

Economically, the period leading up to the war was on the face of it one of success and prosperity: exports more than doubled between 1900 and 1913, but the prosperity was not equally spread and it has been calculated that average real wage rates were 4% lower in 1910 than they had been in 1896[19]. New social security benefits (on the models introduced in Germany by Bismarck 30 years earlier) made up some but not all of the difference.

It was easier, perhaps, to turn your gaze inwards to the cricket field.

---

19   *The Common People 1746-1938*, Cole and Postgate, Methuen, 1938

Chapter Four
Opening Moves

There could possibly have been no cricket in 1914 at all.

In April the cricket ball makers of Kent, where most balls were made and had been made for 150 years, went on strike in a protest against falling pay and their conditions. Highly skilled workers were earning only 30 shillings a week and they sought an increase of five shillings per dozen balls. Their union was the Amalgamated Society of Cricket Ball Makers who, despite the grand name, were essentially confined to the Wisden's, Duke and Readers workshops in Kent which still employed several hundred people, the figure of 200 to 300 being quoted. The manufacturers' original contention was that 'retailers refuse to allow a sufficient margin to allow the payment of a fair wage'.

The *South Eastern Gazette* reported the strike on 21 April: on the same day the *Daily Express* was saying that there was to be a meeting with the employers and an early end to the strike was hoped for.

A.C.MacLaren in *World of Cricket* was disapproving, moaning that the strikers had persuaded the men at Duke's to join and saying that 'to meet the men's demands would cut the manufacturers' profits' unless they could charge an additional 6d a ball. In the 9 May issue Readers had an advert saying that 'owing to the regrettable ball-makers' strike we are unable to announce particulars of the cricket ball we are making for schools, colleges, etc'. By 5 May Dukes had written to the Amalgamated Society of Cricket Ball Makers offering to pay the new rates (which had been agreed) from 31 August.

The Daily Herald (from a rather different perspective) reported on Monday 11 May that 'the cricket ball Bosses are beginning to climb down from their high pedestals. Offering the increase from September rather than 1 January: but the men want it now' and 'success is certain if the men stick to their guns.' It was settled, presumably on those terms.

What this does show is the growing strength of the trade union movement, especially among skilled workers – three-quarters of the workers in the industry were said to be union members. So for the time being cricket went on and at all levels people attended to their various preparations for the season.

The reference to *World of Cricket* is significant. *Cricket*, which had given substantial coverage to the game since 1882, had closed and MacLaren, in partnership with the new proprietor J.N.Pentelow, had launched *World of Cricket* as its successor. It lasted for the one year; whether it would have continued had peace prevailed is another matter.

It has to be remembered that 1914 was not like 1939, and for most people war was nowhere on the horizon. In the first week of May 1914 the county season started fairly slowly, with two games beginning on 2 May. There was no start for first-class cricket in April (let alone March) in those more leisured days. Teams played between 20 and 28 matches in a full season, with the Championship decided on percentages, but, of course, there were no other distractions, and if your best players were picked to play in Gentlemen v Players you carried on with what was left.

It would just be another year of championship cricket with few diversions. Everything seemed normal enough. The 1913 Championship had been won by Kent, who had won 20 of their 28 matches, losing only three. It had been a Championship won by bowlers, with slow left-arm bowler Colin Blythe taking 145 wickets at 15.54. Blythe had retired from international cricket because his nerves couldn't stand it, but he was immensely effective at county level (and indeed at Test level when he could bring himself to play).

The MCC team had returned from South Africa following a Test series won 4-0 (and it was seen as such, with South Africa having been given Test status following the formation of the Imperial Cricket Conference).

That series had been entirely dominated by Sydney Barnes who had taken 49 wickets in four Tests before, entirely typically, refusing to play in the last one after some disagreement about finance. According to an interview he gave many years later the South African authorities had offered to 'pass the hat round' to help with his travel expenses, but had not done so[20]. Being Barnes he would not let it lie and in July we find that he had written to MCC about the matter, but the Committee decided that they were not inclined to put their hands in their pockets either. He had also missed the closing match against Western Province, presumably on his way home, as he had travelled with his wife separately from the rest of the party. Barnes, remarkably enough, was already too old at 41 to be accepted as a volunteer for Kitchener's army, though he would go on taking wickets into the 1930s.

In the meantime an Australian side had condescended to visit New Zealand, wiping up the home team by an innings and 113 runs at Auckland. Four Australians made hundreds, and Victor Trumper, in what was to be his last first-class innings, made 81.

There was no indication at the time that this would be anything other than an ordinary domestic first-class season – no visiting touring side was expected except one from Egypt and the Sudan. Most of their records are now lost, but in July they played an MCC side at Lord's: an MCC side of glittering social cachet but not great cricketing strength who beat them by an innings. And there were two tours from Philadelphia. The Merion Club was touring later in the summer, playing clubs and a couple of county club and ground sides and in June and July there was a tour from Haverford

---

20   Leslie Duckworth, *S.F.Barnes – Master Bowler*, Hutchinson , 1967

College playing against public school sides. Haverford College's website today lists many sports clubs but not, sadly, cricket. The Gentlemen of Philadelphia had toured England with some success in 1908 and Bart King had topped the English bowling averages, but by 1914 Philadelphia cricket was on its last (first-class) legs and nowhere else in the USA counted. There were many reasons for this, but one contributory factor may have been their exclusion from the top table with the formation of the *Imperial* Cricket Conference in 1909.

The second of May, as it happened, was Budget Day: the Budget had been postponed twice and total spending was expected to pass £200 million for the first time, partly due to increasing naval expenditure for the construction of more Dreadnoughts. *The Times* forecast increases in income tax, which would not have been a problem for professional cricketers whose income would in almost all cases have fallen below the threshold, and in any case taxes on earned income had not increased under the Liberals until you reached surtax levels (which the Chancellor was going to set at £3,000 a year). No professional cricketer was going to reach that level (and it seems uncertain whether benefits were taxed at that time – the case of Reed v Seymour, which gave the answer which has prevailed to this day, was not decided until 1927). The *Daily Express*, true to form, had a front-page cartoon showing the taxpayer being squeezed through a mangle.

On 31 March the Advisory County Committee had met at Lord's and agreed (against some opposition) that from 1915 onwards all county championship matches should start on Saturdays and Wednesdays: several counties would try this in 1914. Others saw it as dangerously radical.

At the start of the season County Cricket [is] on Trial, opined *The Times*. It said,' this season sees county cricket trembling in the balance, for without popular support it must die.' It worried about the increasing popularity of football and the fact that you could watch a day's cricket without seeing a result. It continued,

> Cricket is voted dull nowadays because there are not the overwhelming personalities on every county side that spectators have been accustomed to in great matches. With good wickets and "swerve" bowling, first-class cricket of the present day is the dullest of all games unless the spectator really understands the game and takes an intelligent interest in it.

At a more local level, on Wednesday 29 April, the *Derby Evening Chronicle* reported that Mr.G.Curgenven had announced that he would arrive in Britain from British Columbia on Monday and would have time to practise before the county's first match. It referred to him as the "famous" Derbyshire cricketer - a little strong for a man who altogether played 95 games in 20 years. He did, however, play 18 of them in 1914 (with no great success – 565 runs at 18.83). But then the *Victoria Daily Times* in British Columbia reported that he was going back to play as a professional, which would have been sensational if it was true.

In one of those events where there is little more to be said, on 22 April for no good or obvious reason, XIX of Bromley had played XII of England. It was a pretty good England XII at that – Tarrant, Hobbs, James Seymour, Hardinge, Woolley, Douglas, Hitch, Huish, W.Kennedy[21], E.W.Dillon, Fielder, J.T.Hearne – and unsurprisingly won by a wide margin. The match was reported by *World of Cricket* without comment.

But an indicator of the way the wind might blow could be seen in the *Daily Mirror* for 27 April which showed pictures of the FA Cup Final on the front and back pages, together with a match report. Even if it devoted more space to the King than to the football it was a lot more coverage than cricket would get in the *Mirror* where football and boxing were given considerably more space.

The *Manchester Guardian* for 1 May 1914 gives a couple of scores – one is Manchester v Sale (at Old Trafford) and it also mentions the Surrey trial in which J. Howell of Repton made 109. Later in that trial Goatly and Abel apparently scored 168 in 48 minutes for the sixth wicket.

On 2 May *World of Cricket* featured S.J.Pegler who at this time was engaged by Lionel Robinson. Sid Pegler had taken 189 wickets on tour with South Africa in 1912 and would do well again in 1924. In 1914 he played a handful of games for MCC and various gents' pick-up sides, but did take 39 first-class wickets. Though the reference books call him an amateur, he was employed by Robinson whose ground at Old Buckenham in Norfolk was an attempt to improve his social standing. After the war Archie MacLaren filled much the same position as Pegler.

On Saturday 2 May the first ball at the Oval was bowled by Bill Hitch to William Denton of Northamptonshire, one of three brothers who played as amateurs for the county (though J.S.Denton was missing from this game because he had scarlet fever). All survived the war, though Arthur, also not playing in this match, lost a leg. "Bill'itch", as ever the mainstay of Surrey's bowling, had taken 174 wickets in 1913.

The papers of 4 May were reporting on Saturday's play: the novelty of starting games on a Saturday indicated that some counties did have one eye on the spectators.

At another level, on Monday 4 May the *Daily Herald* gave notice that the Daily Herald Cricket Club would begin its fixtures on Wednesday with a match against the District Railway. All newspapers, like most other factories or substantial offices, ran their own cricket teams (and mostly played in leagues).

The Times gave as much weight to the Seniors' matches at Oxford and Cambridge as to the county games, naming the teams for matches commencing that day. The practice was to hold trial matches separately for seniors and freshmen. When it turned to reports in *The Times*, the Seniors' trial matches took priority over the ongoing county games.

---

21   But who was W.Kennedy?

The county season did not exactly begin with a bang. Starting on 2 May, Leicestershire played Essex at Leicester and Surrey played Northamptonshire at the Oval. The *Chelmsford Chronicle* was pleased to welcome the return of Captain W.M.Turner who had not played since 1906 because of his military duties. This season he was to play regularly until the end of July, though overall he played only 46 games for Essex over 27 years. In the second innings for Leicestershire, Sam Coe and Cecil Wood made the first hundreds of the season. Coe was a stalwart professional batsman who had first played for Leicestershire in 1896 and would carry on for a few years after the war, making over 17,000 runs at an average of less than 25. He had appeared for the Players in 1908 in the less prestigious Oval fixture, but his main claim to fame in cricketing folklore was as the first batsman to fall victim to Bosanquet's new mystery ball, the googly, in 1900. Mind you, legend also says that it bounced four times.

Wood's career was remarkably similar in some ways, as he played as a batsman who bowled a bit from 1896 to 1923, but very different in others: he was an amateur (later a coal merchant by trade), though he had played his first Leicestershire season (1896) as a professional. After that he was appointed as the county's Assistant Treasurer so that he could play as an amateur. He had been newly appointed captain for 1914. Both King and Coe, too, had played for London County with W.G.Grace. One wonders just what their relationship was like after all this time. Coe was over 40, Wood just under. After retiring, Coe went on to be the county scorer in the early 30s and continued until 1949. In 1940 Wood became the county secretary. Just to confuse things further, Wood, the amateur, was a stolid opening batsman whereas Coe, the professional, was a dasher.

Also in the Leicestershire side was Alec Skelding, picked as a bowler. Skelding was to carry on for some years, having his best season in 1927 (his benefit year) at the age of 41. and was then for 27 years a first-class umpire. It was John King, though, who won the match for Leicestershire, taking five for 26 as Essex subsided for 129 in their second innings.

At the Oval, remarkably enough, Northamptonshire (then the newest first-class county) had the better of the draw with Surrey. Northants had been performing well above expectations, finishing second in 1912 and fourth in 1913, a performance largely driven by two players, Sydney Smith and George Thompson. Thompson, unusual in that he was a grammar school boy turned professional, had made his debut for the county in 1895 and almost single-handedly dragged the county up to the first-class status it achieved in 1905. Sydney Smith was born in Trinidad of British parents and had toured England with the West Indian team of 1906, doing the double in all matches. A slow left-arm bowler, he had taken six wickets in each innings against Northants and had then stayed to qualify for the county. He captained the county from 1913, was to do the double in 1914 and was one of *Wisden*'s Cricketers of the Year for 1915. In that year he emigrated to New Zealand and subsequently appeared for Auckland and for New Zealand, though before the country was awarded Test status.[22]

---

22   Bill Francis, *Cricket's Mystery Man*, Cricket Publishing Co.Ltd. 2014

With a proper sense of localism the *Chelmsford Chronicle* of 8 May found room to report that O.C.Bristowe of Great Beddow had scored 104* for Christ Church against Trinity College at Oxford. Orme Bristowe in fact played a few games for Essex in 1913 and 1914, chiefly as a leg-break bowler, though 1914 was his last first-class season.

It had been an encouraging start for Leicestershire to win their first game, but immediately after this they went on to play Hampshire at Southampton. Neither county was very strong, having finished tenth and fourteenth respectively in the previous year, but Hampshire actually won this game by an innings and 105 runs, Jaques, Newman and Kennedy bowling Leicestershire out for 134 and 63. Newman and Kennedy would go on carrying the Hampshire bowling for years and years, but Arthur Jaques was an amateur plucked from local club cricket for Hampshire Hogs, a team at the gentlemanly end of things, after failing to get into the XI at Cambridge. He had been born in Shanghai and the 1911 census shows him living on "private means": he volunteered and died at Loos in September 1915.

Hampshire, home to Portsmouth and to Aldershot, had traditionally strong service connections. Lieutenant Cecil Abercrombie, for instance, had played with some success for Hampshire in 1914, but was away on naval duties in 1914 and was to die at Jutland.

Tit-bits, advertising in the *Daily Express* on 4 May, was offering a £1000 prize in a great new easy cricket competition, for placing four champions on one coupon. In the same issue of the *Daily Express* there is amazement at the growth of the FA Cup (500 entries for 1914/15). Interestingly the *Express* too gives the teams in advance for the Cambridge Seniors' Match. In its pre-season rumination it remarked,

> Cricket is British of the British. Other British sports – football, golf, lawn tennis – are making more and more headway abroad and our supremacy therein is being seriously challenged. Not so cricket. It is a game so essentially British that no other nation can approach within measurable distance of us.

One might note that the Empire (or some of it) seems to be included here.

On 5 May *The Times* was reporting, in a mildly paranoid manner, a new bigger and faster German airship: at about the same time there were several reports of airships being seen at night over the eastern counties of England. They seem to have been the UFOs of their day rather than sightings of real airships, and in fact the fear of German invasion and German technology at the time was of much the same sort as the fear of Martian invasion, more titillating than a real threat. That would change, as by 1915 Zeppelin raids on the eastern counties were a reality.

The following day *The Times* tells us that Mr. J.S.F.Morrison had scored 231 in the Seniors' Match at Cambridge, possibly telling the selectors more than they needed to know. He had won his blue in 1912 and had played in early matches for the University in 1913, but before the Lord's match had taken himself off to play for Northumberland. Despite this he was chosen again in 1914, winning another blue. He played on for a while after the war, captaining the university in 1919, then rather confusingly combining Northumberland with Somerset, but played no first-class cricket after 1922, becoming a golf-course architect.

On another front, *The Times* reported on 6 May that Lord Selborne had moved the second reading of the Women's Enfranchisement Bill in the House of Lords, and that the debate had been adjourned, which was basically a piece of blatant parliamentary manoeuvring to kick the Bill into the long grass.

Once again as much attention was paid to the trial matches at the universities as to the county games, and *The Times* on 6 May listed those newly arrived from their public schools who would take part in the Freshmen's trials at Cambridge.

On 8 May *The Times* noticed Mr H.G.Wells' new book *The World Set Free* – a book which opens with an atomic war set in 1956. Wells had by this time written many "scientific romances" of which 1908's *The War in the Air* was going to be the closest to unpleasant reality, though to the Second World War rather than the First. It was all part of a general air of uneasiness.

Aircraft were generally news as the technology was advancing. On 19 May the King and Queen visited the RFC at Aldershot and inspected 25 aircraft, one of them with a wireless installation. The RE1, built by the Royal Aircraft Factory, was commended for its stability, being steered by a single rudder rather than requiring the pilot to control turning and banking simultaneously. Most existing aircraft were unstable as well as hard to fly because in order to be light enough they were vulnerable in the wind.

If that needed any proof, in the same month Mr Gustav Hamel (an Englishman, despite the name), the "foremost exponent in these islands of an art whose military consequence is continually increasing" was lost over the Channel. The next day it was rumoured that he had been picked up by a fishing boat and landed at South Shields, but, unfortunately, it was not true. The life of an airman, even in peacetime, was precarious, and while there was some muttering about foul play there was nothing much in it: he was flying a new aircraft and it was a risky business.

Back to the cricket, and agreement had been reached for an Australian team to tour South Africa, leaving in November.

On 7 May in the MCC v Nottinghamshire game, after G.M.Lee and W.W.Whysall, solid long-serving professionals both, had scored hundreds for the county, Fred Barratt of Nottinghamshire, 20 years old and making his first-class debut, took eight for 91 in the MCC first innings, leading the press to hail "a new fast bowler" who reminded one correspondent of Barnes and 'five times yesterday he broke right across the wicket from leg apparently bowling the off-break action, but none of those magnificent balls got wickets, perhaps because it was too early in the season.' Barratt had been tried in Club & Ground matches in 1913 but was not thought worth taking on the staff; this performance changed minds[23]. He took 100 wickets in 1914 and played with some success until 1931, though his only international recognition was for England in New Zealand in 1929/30, when England are recorded as playing two separate Test series, still leaving most of the best players at home. The comparison with Barnes suggested a wish for a bowler who might be as effective as him but rather more respectful to his social betters.

There was an exhibition billiards match at the Leicester Square Hall, where Inman and Reece were throttling the life out of the game, with the score at close of play Reece 7509 and Inman (in play with a break of 163) 6612. Billiards as a sport was about to collapse under the weight of point scoring, where you might see one player occupying the table for a complete session, and would virtually disappear as a spectator sport, replaced eventually by snooker.

In the Freshman's match at Cambridge L.C.Leggatt (Eton and King's) made 116 and took six for 25 bowling slow leg-breaks. The *Manchester Guardian* was not altogether impressed: it suggested that Leggatt (whose innings took two and a half hours) played a 'cautious game throughout.... He hardly made enough of his physical capabilities.' He played only one first-class match for the University, against Yorkshire, though in June he scored 76 at Lord's for Old Etonians against Old Harrovians in a two-day game.

On Saturday 9 May MCC played Kent and Frank Woolley scored 94 in 75 minutes. At the Oval it was reported to be 'bleak and wintry'. In the Freshmen's match at Oxford Mr M. Howell scored 121 and the bowling of Mr J.Heathcote Amory was commended. Heathcote Amory played a few games for the university in 1914, but after the war played for some years for Devon. Miles Howell returned to Oxford after the war, won a blue again in 1919 and played a while for Surrey. He would also play football for the Corinthians and England Amateurs.

The opening of the season in the Lancashire League saw some low scoring with Church bowled out by Rishton for 20 and Nelson for 29 by Rawtenstall.

There was trouble in the Balkans, but at this point between Greece and Albania, local Greeks having declared the autonomous Republic of Epirus. But there was always trouble in the Balkans and nobody paid much attention.

The Times announced the team for Oxford's opening match, a team containing five Old Etonians. The next day the letters column featured, rather splendidly, letters from Professor A.V.Dicey KC, the Bishop of Zanzibar, Professor Kirsopp Lake, Mr Rollo Appleyard, Professor Silvanus P.Thompson, and Ritter von Pollaky, though not about cricket. None of them was played by Groucho Marx.

On 12 May *The Times* reported the landing of machine guns in Ulster,

---

23   Peter Wynne-Thomas, *Trent Bridge*, Notts CCC 1987

destined for the Ulster Volunteer Force. The police and the customs 'knew nothing of the matter' and apparently cared less.

A report to the London Education Committee advised against the teaching of sex hygiene in elementary schools, but also that teachers should be trained to deal with the 'repression of undesirable habits': they also drew attention to the moral dangers arising from lack of supervision of parks and open spaces.

In the Reichstag the Foreign Office Estimates were being debated. Herr von Jagow, the Foreign Secretary, 'began with the Balkans. The general relief of tension in Europe had progressed.....and he hoped that the regeneration of the Ottoman Empire would be promoted by peace and neighbourliness in the re-distributed territories. He was not happy, though, with the anti-German tone of the Russian press. Negotiations with England 'were being conducted on both sides in the most friendly spirit, a spirit which in other matters also prevailed in Germany's relations with Great Britain.'

In mid-May the committee of the Monmouthshire County Cricket Club held their annual meeting in Newport and, whilst bemoaning a falling-off in gate receipts in Minor County matches at Rodney Parade, they noted an increasing interest in the game in the manufacturing and mining valleys and discussions took place about more matches being staged at Ebbw Vale in order to tap into this growing enthusiasm for the summer game.

Somewhere different in the social scale, among the county scores in *The Times* this day was the scorecard of the annual match between I Zingari and the Household Brigade, played at Chelsea.

Mr F.R.Foster had resigned as captain of Warwickshire but was persuaded during the day to carry on playing. In fact his father had died in April, his elder brother was unwell, and he felt he was needed in the family business; but he agreed to give it one more season[24].

On 18 May *The Times* had an article headed 'The War Cloud', but it was from a correspondent in Belfast. On the railways, the NUR wanted an eight-hour day and a 48-hour week, an increase of 5 shillings for every grade, and full recognition of the union.

At Old Trafford on 16 May Lancashire had experimented with a Saturday start against Derbyshire and had attracted 5,000 spectators. Jack Sharp made 105: then a professional, and a double international who played football for England, he was to reappear after the war as an amateur and eventually as Lancashire's captain. According to Wikipedia, after ten years with Everton he became a director of the club and opened a sports shop (eventually taken over by JJB Sports in the 1980s), but in fact he was advertising his sports store in *World of Cricket* by 1914.

Worcestershire, in the field against Surrey, wore black armbands: it was the day of R.E.Foster's funeral. Foster's death from diabetes at the age of 36 had been noted everywhere: he still held England's record individual

---

24   Robert Brooke, *F.R.Foster*, ACS 2011

score in Tests.

On Tuesday 19 May *The Times* reported that that Warwickshire were looking to acquire the freehold of the Edgbaston ground from Lord Calthorpe for £7,000, paying for it by the issue of debentures. This never happened, though Lord Calthorpe's son Freddie was to become the county captain after the war.

The Times was also very unhappy about the Bill passed for the disestablishment of the Welsh Church, suggesting that whatever the Welsh gained by it, they would fritter it away.

In a further Cambridge trial, Mr L.C.Leggatt, who had already dominated the Freshmen's Trial, made 160*. An Old Etonian, he was to play only game for the University that year, and was to die in action at Pilckem Ridge on 31 July 1917, the opening day of the third battle of Ypres.

On 20 May Sidney Bowkitt, playwright and author of *The Superior Miss Pellender* and *Lucky Miss Dean,* was in court for damaging newspapers belonging to W.H.Smith and assaulting a newsboy. He was bound over for twelve months, having recompensed the boy and vowed to give up his drug habit.

The main cause for real worry was Ulster, where armed opposition to Home Rule from the unionists seemed increasingly likely. *The Times*, like the Tory Party, was inclined to place all the blame on the government. It was also gloomily contemplating the decline of county cricket with attendances falling despite good weather.

At Lord's on 20 May, Sussex were all out for 50 against Tarrant and J.W.Hearne. Tarrant and Hearne were to be two of the names that would recur all season, doing nearly enough with bat and ball to take the title for Middlesex. Frank Tarrant had played for Middlesex since 1904, and for Victoria, his birthplace before and after that. He later played in India and ended up by touring India with an Australian team in 1935/36, by which time he was 55. Though arguably the best all-rounder in the world, he never played Test cricket for Australia because he was based in England. He played for England against The Rest in a Test trial in 1911 and was to take nine for 35 and seven for 34 for "England" against "India" at Bombay in 1915.

"Young Jack" Hearne was not closely related to the numerous other Hearnes (he shared a great-grandfather with the Kentish tribe). His Test record was to be strangely modest for a man who in first-class cricket scored 37,252 runs and took 1,839 wickets.

Neither Tarrant nor Hearne would make *Wisden's* five this year because they had both been there before: Tarrant in 1908 and Hearne in 1912.

At Cambridge Logie Leggatt followed his unbeaten 160 with 67, but it was not enough to get him into the team against Sussex.

If Ulster was the real worry, the suffragettes were ever present. It was reported that the WSPU – the miltant suffragettes – proposed to send a delegation to meet the King at Buckingham Palace – and that if Mrs Pankhurst was to lead the delegation, the police would re-arrest her under the "Cat and Mouse" Act.

On the following day Mrs Pankhurst, along with others, was indeed arrested for taking part in what *The Times* called 'a suffragist riot' outside Buckingham Palace. The *Manchester Guardian* reported that 1,500 police were on duty and that only one of the protesters managed to get as far as the main gates, where she was arrested. Then: 'A huge Inspector plucked Mrs Pankhurst out of the struggling group and ran away with her in his arms into the clear space in front of the Palace'. Then on 23 May it was reported that the National Gallery and the Wallace Collection had been closed until further notice because of attacks by suffragists. There had also been "uproar" at a theatrical performance attended by the King and Queen. Later in the month *The Times* also reported "suffragist brawling at St Paul's" when a woman tried to mount the pulpit and address the congregation. The WSPU's low-level terrorism – always aimed at property not people – was highly successful in calling attention to their grievances but did not appear to win them support or to bring the prospect of women's suffrage any closer.

On the cricket field Philip Mead scored 213 for Hampshire against Yorkshire. His main support was from an innings of 76 by Lieutenant G.C.Harrison, an Old Etonian and another of Hampshire's endless supply of military men with a bit of time on their hands. Gerald Harrison played briefly after the war, but his first-class career was over by 1920.

Somerset v Surrey at Bath moved at some speed and by the end of the first day Somerset had made 77 and 104-8, Surrey 104. For some reason lost in the mists of time Hobbs (always "John" rather than Jack to *World of Cricket*) opened the bowling in Somerset's first innings but was not a wicket-taker. Somerset lost the match but used only two bowlers, the young "Farmer" White and Ernie Robson. W.J.Abel's 34 was the highest score of the match.

On 21 May in a two-day match at Lord's, MCC and Ground scored 538-6 declared (J.W.Hearne, having a rest from first-class cricket, 228) and bowled the Minor Counties out for 146: not bad for a day's play.

Hampshire's hopes of beating Yorkshire were foiled by a partnership of 312 by Denton and Hirst, a new fourth-wicket record for the county.

On Monday 25 May the front page of *The Times* carried a full page advertisement for *Rhodesia the Land of Sunshine.* Not to be outdone, Vickers Ltd took the whole of page 8, proclaiming that they could design, build, engine and arm all kinds of warships. This was a 48-page edition, most of it devoted to the Empire (with ample space given to articles about the major advertisers).

It was reported from Vienna that the Emperor Francis Joseph was now recovering after eight weeks of catarrh and bronchitis.

There was a big first-wicket partnership for Middlesex on 23 May. "Good batting by Mr Anson and Tarrant," said *The Times*, punctilious as ever about the social niceties. At the end of the first day at Leyton Middlesex (put in to bat) were 245-1: they went on to 464-1 before declaring, Tarrant, 250* and J.W.Hearne 106*, and then bowled Essex out for 173 and 235: 'Young Jack' Hearne adding 14 wickets to his hundred.

In 1912 and 1913 Essex had won only three matches and lost 17, in both seasons finishing 15th out of 16 in the championship. These were the worst two seasons of their first-class life so far. They had begun 1914 where they left off, with consecutive heavy defeats by Leicestershire, Sussex and Yorkshire. Then came Middlesex, the worst of all. But under the captaincy of Johnny Douglas Essex, launching their policy of touring the county with games at Southend and Colchester, were to improve dramatically.

On 26 May there was a substantial advertisement in *The Times* for the new Wolseley Torpedo Phaeton (with electrical lighting equipment). Wolseley at this time was owned by Vickers, an early conglomerate. This would have set you back £475.

From Paris it was reported that M. Clement Bayard, a constructor of airships, had been arrested in Cologne, apparently for watching the descent of a Zeppelin. The headline is 'German Spy Mania'.

One could look through the theatrical announcements. The Royal Opera House had a formidable look – Montemezzi's *L'amore dei tre re* tonight, *Un ballo in maschera* tomorrow, *Rigoletto* on Friday (with Melba herself), *Aida* on Saturday, Shaw's *Pygmalion* at His Majesty's, the 425th performance of *Kismet* at the Globe (produced by Oscar Asche, a keen but untalented cricketer himself). And far more: you would have to admit that the intellectual level was slightly higher than the West End manages today (and, too, there were more theatres to choose from and that without counting the music halls).

At this point, towards the end of May, it is interesting to see how many military men were turning out for various sides, MCC and Ground v Hampshire involved four, Major Fulton turned out for Worcestershire and the Household Brigade were playing Harrow.

In the matches that finished on 27 May, the main news was that Surrey beat Yorkshire at Bradford by 28 runs in a game which changed throughout. Yorkshire, chasing 223, were 106 for 8, but Hirst and Birtles added 82 for the ninth wicket to take Yorkshire close. On the first day Jack Hobbs, opening with Hayward, had scored 100 out of 151 in 75 minutes with 11 fours and five sixes, but, despite that and 125 from Hayes, Surrey were dismissed for 317. Hobbs in 1914 at the age of 31 not only scored heavily but fast and was perfectly happy to hit the ball in the air. This was his first hundred of the season after a quiet start: he had given a hostage to fortune in 1913 by writing a book called *How To Make A Century*[25]. Wilfred Rhodes took six for 109 in 24 overs, quite unusually rough treatment for him, though he obviously had his revenge, adding five for 56 in the second

---

25   J.B.Hobbs, *How To Make A Century*, A&C Black, 1913

innings.

Middlesex and Worcester started on 27 May and Frank Tarrant scored 200 as the county piled up 477-6 on the first day. As he was fresh from scoring 250* against Essex at Leyton, this was quite a feat.

The next day *The Times* reported a speech by Sir Edward Carson in Wales – a speech in which he referred to the arms now held by the Ulster Unionists. Carson was sailing close to the wind here, and most of the Tory party was sailing with him, having given at least tacit support to the mutiny at the Curragh which made it clear that the Army could not be relied on in Ulster. Armed defiance of the law was clearly on his agenda: *The Times*, need it be said, was cheering him on.

In London Dr M.A.Low demonstrated the new wonder of the age, transmitting pictures by wire and forecasting that it would be possible to send pictures wirelessly. *The Times* was capable of believing many things, but this was a step too far, surely.

A letter from "NCK", addressing the problems of county cricket, put them down to averages and the insistence on a championship. His solution was the abolition of the championship, fewer matches, and more amateurs.

Mind you, there were tougher sports than cricket. The 1914 Giro d'Italia is regarded as the hardest cycle race of all time, with 400 kilometre stages in appalling weather; 81 started and 8 finished. The British press took no notice (as would be the case for nearly 100 years).

Mr C.E.S.Rucker achieved a hat trick for Oxford University against MCC, the second of five first-class matches he played for the University in a short career. Charles Rucker returned after the war as secretary of the club, but had lost a leg in the war and his cricketing days were over.

The paper on 1 June was full of the loss of the *Empress of Ireland*, sunk in fog in the Saint Lawrence on her way from Quebec to Liverpool after a collision with a Norwegian collier with the loss of over a thousand lives. The loss of life was on the same scale as that of the *Titanic* but the passenger list was less distinguished. Legend has it that the ship's cat, Emmy, refused to board her and could not be coaxed aboard, watching her leave from the roof of Pier 27.

Against Warwickshire on 29 May Jack Hobbs made 183 in 170 minutes, and Frank Foster's 29 overs cost him 149 runs, though he did eventually clean bowl Hobbs. Percy Fender made 140, also at better than a run a minute, and Surrey on the second day scored 494 in under five hours on the way to winning by an innings and 197. On the same day Kent dealt out much the same treatment to Leicestershire, adding 408 in less than four and a half hours, including three centuries. Lancashire had been playing Essex at Old Trafford and Alfred Hartley, an amateur who had played fairly regularly until 1912, and had even been one in *Wisden*'s five in 1911, played his only county match of the season. Hartley, born in New Orleans, died in France in October 1918.

On 30 May Frank Tarrant's benefit match began, but his run of scores did not continue as he was out for nine against Hampshire (though he had earlier taken four wickets).

The averages at this point (published no doubt to the disgust of NCK) showed Tarrant unsurprisingly top of the batting, with 821 runs at 81.22. Top of the bowling, with 18 wickets at 11.06, was "Slater" (Archie Slater of Derbyshire) though Tarrant, having the benefit season from heaven, had taken 41 at 16.85.

The Times also published the championship table: the figures depended on percentages as not all counties played the same number of games. Middlesex had played three and won three, so were top. Hampshire, remarkably, were second with three wins and a win on first innings in their first four games (though two of the wins had been against Leicestershire). Surrey had won five out of six, though.

The Times also reported a win for Eton against "Liverpool" in a one-day match. All, it seemed, was as it should be.

Chapter Five

June 1914

On 2 June *The Times* was reporting a political crisis in France, where an election had been held and had produced a landslide for parties of the left which took 475 of 601 seats in the Assembly (though they didn't necessarily talk to each other). Monsieur Doumerge had originally taken office, but felt that his job was merely to get things organised and so resigned. The various parties of the left were circling round each other.

On the same day the parish church at Wargrave, near Henley, was burnt to the ground: militant suffragettes appeared to be responsible.

It was Whit weekend and on the Monday there were about 10,000 spectators at Bramall Lane, Sheffield, for the Roses Match. Yorkshire batted all day and made 381, the highest score being Roy Kilner's 93: Kilner played for Yorkshire until 1927, dying in the following spring from enteric fever contracted in India. For Lancashire, James Tyldesley managed six for 129. *Wisden* tells us that he 'died in a nursing home in Bolton while under an anaesthetic'. A reminder, perhaps, that there were other tragedies than war.

On 3 June *The Times* had reported the continuation of a hearing of charges against five suffragists: they were charged with being persons having committed or being about to commit a felony and also conspiring together to commit malicious damage to property. Also reported was an arson attempt near Market Harborough and a charge of insulting conduct against some young men who had tried to break up a suffragist meeting and throw the women into a pond: they were discharged and warned but the magistrate was more concerned by the behaviour of the women. It is clear that the behaviour of the suffragists and especially their refusal to behave themselves in court worried the establishment as much as what they had done.

For Leicestershire against Northamptonshire Sammy Coe had made an unbeaten 252, a county record until beaten by Phil Simmons in 1994 (and subsequently by Brad Hodge and Hylton Ackerman). It remains the highest score made for Leicestershire by an English player. It was not, however, the highest score in this round of matches as Frank Foster made 305* for Warwickshire against Worcestershire.

For Marlborough against Liverpool (again, the scores given in *The Times*) three young batsmen scored centuries in a total of 451. J.R.Barnes was to go on to play first-class cricket for Lancashire for some years, though he was not always available as he was a cotton merchant. R.D.Busk played a couple of games for Hampshire in 1919 and then played regularly for

Dorset. R.C.Ashfield is known to have played once after the war for a weak Cambridge University side that lost to Liverpool and District in 1920. At least all of them survived the war.

At Dudley Warwickshire had won massively and Field returned figures of 8.4-6-2-6. His figures would not read so well nowadays, as he bowled five no-balls.

Yorkshire and Lancashire, in classic fashion, made no attempt to obtain a result. The first innings of both sides had occupied nearly two days, with Yorkshire holding a small lead. Lancashire had made 370 with James Tyldesley and W.Huddleston putting on 141 for the ninth wicket. It was Bill Huddleston's highest score: he had taken 100 wickets for the only time in 1913, but he was 41 and did not reappear after the war, though he continued to play with considerable success for Leigh, his club side. Yorkshire declared at 299-4 in their second innings and Lancashire made no attempt to make 311 in 190 minutes. Mr A.H.Hornby, opening the batting, made 45*. He was the Lancashire captain and the son of "Monkey" Hornby.

'There was great excitement at Taunton' as Somerset actually won a match against Gloucestershire, making 134-3 in 90 minutes, Bertram Bisgood making 78*. He was an amateur who played on and off for Somerset between 1907 and 1921: one of that class who had not attended a major public school, having been to Prior Park College in Bath, which had been established in 1830 and had been intended to be the country's first Catholic university: it is still there, occupying a spectacular Palladian mansion. He was a solicitor by profession and in 1911 had been living in Richmond, Surrey, but he had been born in Somerset.

On 4 June *The Times* carried a list of malicious damage to property carried out by militant suffragettes, divided into damage to works of art, bomb explosions and 'incendiary outrages' including the destruction of Yarmouth Pier and the burning of the Bath Hotel in Felixstowe, the grandstand at Birmingham racecourse and several country houses. The paper also reported that a procession of suffragettes in Bournemouth was attacked by a crowd. This was a serious campaign indeed and certainly today would be described as terrorism.

The Times was suggesting that the authorities now had a full list of subscribers to the WSPU and that they could be held responsible for the damage, and alleged that that much of this was being done by women who were 'well paid' to do it.

Worse than that! A correspondent opined, 'One gentleman writes in this morning's Times under the name of "Anti-Rot". He is against killing animals by shooting or hunting them to death, and says he would rather teach his son to hit a golf ball than shoot a bird. We all know the end of that boy, and Anti-Rot will only have himself to blame.'

Mr R.H.Lyttleton wrote today to argue for a change in the LBW law because of the number of high-scoring draws. It was perhaps unfortunate that the letter appeared next to the account of Kent being bowled out for 86 by Northamptonshire (who then replied with 141 all out by the close). William Wells, professional and fast-medium bowler, took seven for 39: he was to carry on playing for Northants until 1926. Kent recovered from this to win by a substantial margin, Colin Blythe taking seven for 15 to bowl out Northants for 57 in their second innings.

C.B.Fry turned out for Hampshire in his first game for two years, scoring 41 against Gloucestershire; in the second innings he made 112. Equal prominence in *The Times* was given to Eton College v Eton Ramblers – the Ramblers scored 493 but were unable quite to force victory. Kenneth Nicholl, who had captained the Eton XI in 1903, scored a century as did G.H.G.M.Cartwright, later President of the Ramblers until his death in 1976.

Lancashire were playing Nottinghamshire without James Tyldesley who was 'required by his local club for the weekend' – employed as a professional at a Lancashire League club: he was certainly playing for Ramsbottom in 1915.

Hubert Garrett was making his only first-class appearance of the season for MCC against Cambridge University with no particular success, after turning out for Somerset throughout July 1913. Australian-born, he was to die at Gallipoli.

On 8 June the whole front page of *The Times* was taken up by an advertisement for W.Vernon & Sons 'Millennium' flour. Indeed the whole issue seems to have been about food and drink with many advertisers taking full pages. It was a surprise to come across a reference to '"the curd now fashionable as yagourt"'.

When you finally come to the cricket scores on page 58, we see that Mr J.S.F.Morrison had scored 75 and 233* for Cambridge University against MCC. So perhaps that is why he was forgiven for having gone off to play for Northumberland the previous year. The innings also hoisted him into the top ten in the national batting averages, now headed by Frank Foster after his triple century. The bowling averages were now led by Bill Fairservice of Kent (who played until 1921 and then for a few years for Northumberland), and Middlesex, with four wins in five matches, topped the early Championship table.

On 9 June it was reported that M Ribot had agreed to try to form a government in France. He indeed formed a ministry, but it lasted only four days. There were worries about Mexico and in the Balkans where Greece was proposing to buy battleships. Greece and the Ottoman Empire were conducting their own mini-Dreadnought contest, some of it with other people's cast-offs.

The following day *The Times* reported what a very sound government M Ribot had put together. There was a general strike in Rome. There was a grand state ball at Buckingham Palace, with a full list of those attending, including substantial numbers of minor German royalty as well as all the ambassadors from everywhere. For once it would seem that security had been tight enough to keep the suffragettes out (many of them were well-brought-up girls who had been presented at court in their time).

It was beginning to be possible to keep an eye on the Championship and Surrey were unceremoniously thumped by Essex at the Oval. Johnny Douglas with 74*, followed by 11 wickets in the match for 98, bowled unchanged through both innings with Bert Tremlin, a medium-pacer having his best season at the age of 37: he carried on for a year or two after the war before becoming a first-class umpire. Middlesex, in a game starting a day later, were in a useful position against Warwickshire with a small first-innings lead, but on the next day Tarrant rampaged through Warwickshire's batting on a wet but drying pitch to bowl them out for 69 and Middlesex needed only 27 to win. Middlesex now looked in a strong position, having won five games out of six.

Michael Falcon, mostly of Norfolk, took 13 in the match for the Free Foresters against Cambridge University, though Cambridge in the end won by one wicket.

MCC had written to the South African Cricket Association apologising for any apparent discourtesy that had been offered to the Mayor and citizens of Bloemfontein during the winter tour. The art of the grudging and minimal apology was already in place.

On 11 June an argument about the place of the battleship in modern warfare was raging. Sir Percy Scott argued that submarines and aircraft were making the battleship redundant. Scott had retired from the Navy with the rank of Admiral in 1913. His ideas may have been premature, but battleships played very little part in the war when it came. Scott was well known as a maverick, but this idea was truly shocking as an absolute faith in the Royal Navy was essential to every true-born Englishman (and because the country had just spent and was still spending an enormous amount of money on battleships).

On June a bomb went off in Westminster Abbey, causing some damage to the coronation chair. Two women who happened to be around were arrested but then released. On the same day the *Manchester Guardian* reported that in Portsmouth two suffragettes were chased by a brick-throwing mob and a meeting broken up in great disorder.

The Times reported the inquest into the death of Miss Joan Lavender Guthrie: she had been a militant suffragette and had been in prison in 1912. After that she left home and went on the stage under the name of Laura Gray. She had become addicted to alcohol and drugs, went to night-clubs and was 'leading an immoral life'. She was pregnant. The coroner 'commented strongly on the effect of militancy on her ill-balanced mind.' Somehow the assumptions about cause and effect summed up the mindset of the conservative part of middle-class England.

At Lord's on 11 June Middlesex were playing Yorkshire and had scored 170-5 when rain set in. Surrey on the same day completed a win over

Leicestershire. Tom Rushby was the bowler here, taking 11 wickets in the match. He was another who played on after the war until 1921. Hampshire, at this point high in the table, had a splendid day against Somerset at Bath. Jaques and Kennedy bowled Somerset out for 83 and by the close Hampshire were 232-7, with Mead unbeaten on 110. Philip Mead played on for Hampshire until 1936, making the most runs for a single team in cricket history, with a couple of years for Suffolk after that.

The military seem to have been much occupied by cricket. Cambridge University were due to play the Army, though *The Times* reports that the title of the team was changed to The Navy and Army: it was not a very strong team (no suggestions that this was because of calls to duty) and at lunch was 63-7, at which point it rained.

The Times also reports a game in which the Royal Artillery beat the Household Brigade.

There was a meeting of the various county secretaries at Lord's to arrange the fixtures for 1915, and it was generally agreed that matches would start on Wednesdays and Saturdays, with some flexibility for bank-holiday weekends.

On 13 June *The Times* reported that in France, M Ribot's "ministry of all the talents" had fallen at the first hurdle, being defeated on its first appearance in the Assembly. It was thought that M Viviani, who sat as an independent socialist, would be next in line.

The first feature on the cricket page this day was a preview of Old Etonians v Old Harrovians, even though it was scheduled for two days and so not first-class.

Hampshire had bowled out Somerset for 38 in their second innings, Arthur Jaques finishing with match figures of 14 for 54. Mr S.H.Saville, who later in the year would turn out for Middlesex, made 141* against the Army (the name of the side apparently changed back again). As the Army side included a Reverend and three Misters, it was perhaps not as military as it might have been. It is, of course, possible that the Misters were Lieutenants/2nd Lieutenants and the Reverend an Army Chaplain, Mr Walter Parke, who opened the batting and whose only first-class match this was, was to die in France in October. For Harry Gardner too it was his only first-class appearance and the Rev John Burrough had not played much first-class cricket since he won his blue for Cambridge in 1895. It would seem that that the Army had turned up short and picked up what players they could. If duty was calling, it might have been because of Ireland, but nothing to do with the European situation.

After the second day Middlesex had gained a first-innings lead of 98 against Yorkshire – 277 against 179 – but with only a day to go would have to work to force a win.

A team had been picked for Rest of England against the team that had toured South Africa – described as the 'Centenary at Lord's' (the centenary being that of the current ground). C.B.Fry would captain the side.

It was reported that a dog at Mannheim, named Rolf, was credited with answering theological questions and doing little sums correctly, having originally been discovered helping the children with their maths homework.

At Lord's caution prevailed, Warner declining to set a reasonable target, and Yorkshire, left to make 271 in 140 minutes, declined the invitation.

Surrey started a new game, against Essex at Leyton (before a crowd of 6,000): Essex were all out for 309.

15 June was a considerable day for batting – Tarrant became the first to reach 1,000 runs for the season in the course of an innings of 198, Middlesex scoring 427-2 against Lancashire at Lord's. Surrey scored 381 to take a lead against Essex – Hobbs made 215*, taking 22 off an over from Tremlin. Crowther Charlesworth, the Warwickshire professional, made 206 out of a total of 353-6 against Yorkshire.

The teams were announced for the match between the Royal Navy and the Army, which would begin at Lord's on 25 June as part of the centenary celebrations.

On 16 May Middlesex roared on to 501-3 before declaring – J.W.Hearne's 204 saw him the second man to reach 1,000 for the season. In reply Lancashire scored 238 and, following on, 32-1. At Leyton, Hitch and Rushby bowled Essex out for 197 and Surrey won by seven wickets. Lord Harris wrote to *The Times* to say that there was nothing wrong with the game and no need therefore to do anything about the LBW law or to worry about the county finances.

England beat America at polo in the second "test", having already won the first. The English team were all officers, the Americans were just millionaires.

On 17 June the National Union of Railwaymen, meeting at Swansea, adopted a programme demanding an eight-hour-day and an all-round increase of five shillings a week. There was some criticism from the membership, but that was for not including a demand for a minimum wage of 30 shillings a week. They were also to approve the formation of the Triple Alliance with the Miners' Federation and the Transport Workers' Federation. *The Times* was shocked to discover that some of the speakers in the debate appeared to be Socialists. Interestingly, though, the paper was inclined to back the marine engineers in another ongoing strike, remarking that for such skilled men the demands were on the low side.

At Lord's Middlesex were unable to force victory against Lancashire as they batted through for 397-7, Jack Sharp 128 and Ernest Tyldesley 94.

Oxford University beat G.J.V.Weigall's XI by an innings: Bill Ashdown, a Kent stalwart for years after the war, made his first-class debut for Weigall's XI at the age of 15. He was to appear in a festival match at Harrogate in 1947, the only player to straddle both wars.

Westminster drew with Radley, W.G.Le Doux Veitch making 118 for

Westminster. He died on 4 August 1916, a Second Lieutenant in the Royal Sussex Regiment, still only aged 19.

In the championship Middlesex (five wins out of eight) were still top, Surrey (seven out of ten) were second and, no doubt to their great surprise, Hampshire, who had just beaten the champions, Kent, were third with five out of nine.

The next day Miss Sylvia Pankhurst turned up at Westminster where (according to *The Times*) she intended to starve to death at the entrance to the House of Commons unless she was met by the Prime Minister, but he agreed to meet a delegation of six women from the East End, and Miss Pankhurst returned home to be arrested again.

At Nottingham on 18 June Middlesex dismissed the home county for 190, but slipped to 39-4 themselves, though Tarrant was unbeaten on 25. Essex, with seven amateurs in the side, played Worcestershire at Castle Park, Colchester. It was the first time that they had played there and they scored 381-7, Captain W.M.F.Turner making 84. Hampshire scored 239 against Surrey at the Oval, the captain, E.M.Sprot, making 131. Sprot was one of those over-accomplished amateurs: he won the Army Rackets Challenge Cup, was a good golfer, a keen shot and fisherman and a noted billiards player, though by now he was 42.

The first cricket report for 19 June was, of course, the Old Etonians v Old Harrovians match which took priority over county matches as far as *The Times* was concerned. Peter Johnson, a New Zealander who played for many years for Somerset, made 102 and Logie Leggatt 76. At the Oval Hobbs scored 163 in three and a half hours and Arthur Jaques bowled leg theory with only one fielder on the off side. Middlesex were two runs behind Notts on first innings. Notts reached 157-5 in their second innings at the close.

Mr J.A.Sanger made 102 for Cheltenham against Marlborough. Sanger was to play for Lord's Schools this year, but played only minor cricket after the war.

By 20 June Essex had won at Colchester, with nine wickets in the match for G.B.Davies – six for 51 in the second innings. Geoffrey Davies was still at Cambridge, but the University had a break between matches and he turned out for Essex instead. Davies, regarded as academically brilliant as well as a fine cricketer, died in the Battle of Loos in 1915.

On Monday 22 June the birthday honours list was announced. There was an earldom for Lord Kitchener, J.G.Frazier, author of *The Golden Bough*, was made a baronet. Joseph Cook, the Liberal Prime Minister of Australia (though he had started in the Labour Party) became a Privy Councillor: he had begun his working life as a coal miner in Staffordshire.

Mr Asquith had received his delegation from the East London Federation of Suffragists and said that their arguments should have 'careful and mature consideration', and agreed to consider the release of Sylvia Pankhurst. The *Manchester Guardian* said, 'of all the many talks on the suffrage that

Mr Asquith has had with suffragists, today's was the most intimate and probably the most interesting' as he spoke to ordinary working women rather than the well-to-do. It is difficult now to understand how fearful politicians were about this issue – New Zealand had given women the vote as long ago as 1893.

There was severe rioting in Andover, with the rioters only dispersed by a charge of mounted police, with some 2,000 people involved: the latest word was that police were still dealing with groups and the mayor was preparing to read the Riot Act. Such civil unrest was unusual.

The Times called it a fateful week, with the situation in Ireland still deteriorating and (in their view) the government doing nothing about it.

On the cricket field the Eton and Harrow Old Boys' match was drawn (it had only been allotted two days which was unlikely to be enough). A fair number of gentlemen had preferred it to turning out for their county sides, including B.J.T.Bosanquet, A.C.MacLaren and L.H.Tennyson.

Hampshire hung on for a draw at the Oval, with a century from H.A.W.Bowell, a long-serving professional from 1902 to 1927. His eventual career average was 24.13 but he scored 18,466 runs for the county. Such men were the backbone of the county game. Derbyshire scored 401-6 against Northants with 124 from Leonard Oliver, formerly of Manchester Grammar School. It was his first hundred though he had been playing since 1908. He played until 1924 and his career average was 20.39. This perhaps draws attention to those amateurs who were not by any means gentlemen of leisure – Oliver appears in the 1911 census as an ironmonger and plumber, working with his father and brother.

Kent beat Yorkshire by an innings and 149 runs at Tonbridge: Middlesex, still unbeaten, won at Trent Bridge, chasing down 233-4 in about three hours. Mr William Robertson – an Old Harrovian, not picked for their team this year, though he did appear for them in 1920 – made 130 in just over two hours.

At this stage in the season J.W.Hearne, Tarrant, Hobbs, Mead and Woolley were all averaging over 50 – Tarrant had also taken 73 wickets at 17.01.

The Australian team to tour South Africa was announced, though a number of leading players were unable to tour, including Victor Trumper. Five of the nominated team never played Test cricket, though one of them, A.G.Moyes, went on to become one of Australia's best cricket writers.

The Times editorial on 23 June was headed 'the last hope of peace' and related (of course) to Ireland. *The Times* suggested that it might be for the opposition to try framing a settlement, though, since the opposition was mostly egging on Ulster to rebellion, that seemed an improbable scenario.

Following the riots in Andover one man was brought to court for breaking a window, but the case collapsed as the house owner refused to be a witness, saying he hadn't seen who did it and it was only one shilling's worth of damage anyway.

The centenary match at Lord's, starting on 22 June, was effectively the biggest game of the season in a year with no Tests, with over 8,000 people watching. The Rest of England, batting against the MCC side that had toured South Africa, probably found life easier as Barnes had withdrawn with a strained thigh. The Rest scored 382-5 on the first day, several batsmen making it past 50 but only Edward "Punter" Humphreys of Kent getting to three figures.

Cambridge University were playing H.D.G.Leveson Gower's XI and did not bat very well, though Geoffrey Davies scored 92. At Horsham Hampshire scored 374-9, with Bowell managing another hundred. Yorkshire, not apparently themselves this season, were bowled out for 164 by Leicestershire at Bradford. *The Times* also gave the full score for the Household Brigade against the Band of Brothers at Burton Court, part of the grounds of the Royal Chelsea Hospital.

On the second day at Lord's the King turned up with the Prince of Wales and Prince Albert: there was some rain early on but then the Rest took their score to 467 and bowled the touring team out for 94, Hitch taking seven for 42. By the close, having followed on the tour team had lost Hobbs in taking the score to 60-1. At Horsham Alec Kennedy took six for 49 to bowl Sussex out for 146 in reply to Hampshire's 396.

In the middle of the game at Lord's the MCC held a centenary dinner for 250 people, presided over by Lord Hawke. The list, dripping with peers, was headed by Prince Albert of Schleswig-Holstein. Prince Albert served in the Prussian Army though his elder brother Christian Victor had joined the British army. Albert was excused front-line duties against Britain during the war and spent it on the headquarters staff in Berlin. Lord Hawke proposed the toast of 'Lord's Cricket Ground and the MCC'. He regretted that the Press published the averages so often since it led to batsmen playing for their averages and so to slow cricket, and forecast the end of the tea interval since the public disliked it: but he believed that 'unfair bowling had been banished from the game for all time', which was perhaps optimistic.

On 25 June it was noted that King Peter of Serbia was about to undergo a cure at the baths at Vranya and had passed responsibility to the Crown Prince Alexander. It had initially been reported that King Peter had abdicated – in which case Alexander might have faced a challenge from his elder brother Prince George. *The Times* commented that 'a more inauspicious moment for the transfer of the royal dignity could hardly be imagined', which was rapidly to turn out a great deal truer than they could have realised.

There had been severe rioting in Italy, apparently formented by anarchists. Errico Malatesta was accused by *The Times* of being a ringleader: he was, in fact, living in London and ran an electrical workshop in Islington.

On the cricket field the MCC South African team did better at the second attempt but still went down by an innings and 190. Bill Hitch took another five wickets to give him twelve in the match. Sussex had fought back well at Horsham, setting Hampshire 80 to win. They did it but lost eight wickets in the process, Vincett and Mr N.J.Holloway bowling unchanged. Holloway was a Cambridge blue who carried on playing for Sussex after the war, though rather occasionally. His brother Bernard, who also played a few games for Sussex but was better known as a rugby player, was to die at Loos in September 1915. John Vincett was a professional who turned amateur after the war, playing for Sussex in 1919 and then turning out in a couple of games for Surrey in 1921.

Cambridge beat Mr Leveson Gower's XI by eight runs at Eastbourne, somewhat aided by the fact that Mr Leveson Gower himself and also Mr C.U.Peat had absented themselves at the end of the game. The score had been 133-2 but fell to 165-8, at which point the side ran out of batsmen. It would seem that the two had taken themselves off believing that the match was drawn, though Mr Leveson Gower might not have gone far as his XI was going to play Oxford the next day on the same ground.

The Times ruminated at length about the strength of the Oxford XI. It is clear that the newspaper regarded the Oxford and Cambridge matches as more interesting to its readers than the county games. The paper had been acquired by Lord Northcliffe in 1908, but there was no suggestion that it was looking for a popular readership.

On 25 June Lady Randolph Churchill's political play, *The Bill*, was produced at the Prince of Wales's Theatre. The play dealt with a Liberal attempt to bring forward a bill for universal suffrage which might have been topical enough, but the paper seems to suggest that the audience was made up of her friends.

There was a great fancy-dress midnight ball at the Savoy in aid of the National Institute for the Blind (a cause being driven by Arthur Pearson of the *Daily Express*). Among the glittering array of guests was Prince Paul of Serbia, the King's nephew and later Regent of Yugoslavia at the outbreak of the Second World War. There was Jarrett's famous Coon Band from New York and there were two American Bars selling cocktails.

As far as *The Times* was concerned, the leading cricket match of the day was the Royal Navy against the Army at Lord's. On the first day the Navy scored 380 and the Army 6-0. It had first-class status, though only eight of the 22 ever played first-class cricket for a county – five of them for Hampshire, always reliant on military connections at Aldershot or Portsmouth. Perhaps surprisingly, only two of the 22 were to die in the war.

Haverford College from Philadelphia began their tour but had not yet got their land legs, being bowled out by Shrewsbury for 68 and losing by 202 runs. Somerset were beaten by an innings and 127 by Northamptonshire; it was only too easy.

On 28 June *The Times* reported on the arrest at Kiel of the 78-year-old Lord Brassey, suspected of spying on the Imperial Dockyards. He did not stay in custody long – especially since he was due that evening to have dinner with the Kaiser – but perhaps it is indicative of the general sense of paranoia.

The leading counties were not playing in this round, but Frank Woolley made a fine 117 for Kent against Leicestershire. Yorkshire's troubles continued, Notts at the close of the second day being 287 ahead with four second-innings wickets left. That was all *The Times* had to say, as compared with long accounts of the Royal Navy v The Army, Mr Leveson Gower's team's innings win over Oxford and the first day of Eton v Winchester.

On Monday 29 June *The Times* reported the assassination of the Archduke Franz Ferdinand and his wife at Sarajevo. The paper thought that this might lead to difficulties for the Slavs, and was sympathetic to the Emperor himself. There was no suggestion and no reason to suppose that this was in any way a critical event for the rest of Europe. The British royal family postponed a state ball and ordered a week's mourning. On the back page of the *Daily Mirror* on Saturday 4 July is a picture of Gavrilo Princip being led away by Austrian guards, but for the *Mirror*, the main story occupying most of three issues, was the death of Joseph Chamberlain. Chamberlain's greatest achievements were in municipal Birmingham, but it was the notion of Imperial Preference that appealed to the owner of the *Mirror*.

The *Daily Mirror* was not tremendously interested in sport. It had originally been intended as a paper for women: its main selling point now was its pictures (which included many of young women frolicking on beaches). Its cricket scores were a mixture of full and summarised scores, taking second or third place to racing and boxing. Of course betting had been illegal since 1906: the publication of runners and riders (and odds) in detail indicates that it was very much alive. Every factory had its bookie's runner.

Some of the regional papers seemed to take the news from the Balkans more seriously. The assassination dominated the Welsh papers the following morning, with stories of further Suffragette disturbances in Hyde Park and at Llandaff Cathedral sidelined as the newspaper editors focussed their attention on events in Sarajevo. 'There is no longer any doubt that the crime was the result of a pan-Servian plot' wildly proclaimed the *Western Mail*, 'conceived with diabolical cunning and carried out with callous determination'. For the next few days, the same paper carried details of the funeral arrangements in Vienna, as well as news that the Secretary of the Austro-Hungarian Legation at Belgrade had sent a despatch to Vienna accusing Serbia of complicity in the assassination.

On 29 June the *Derby Evening Telegraph* published the scores of Repton School v Old Reptonians (Repton, of course, being the local Public School). J.Howell made 202* for the school (it remained a school record for 94 years). Howell, the school captain, played for Surrey 2nd XI and the Public Schools in August, scoring 82 and 78* for the Rest against Lord's Schools. He died in Flanders on 25 September 1915, just 20 years old and another Second Lieutenant. *Wisden* said of him that he was 'potentially an England batsman' and that 'among all the young cricketers who have fallen during the war, not one of brighter promise than John Howell can be named'.

The Tsar and his family visited Admiral Beatty's flagship, the *Lion*, at Kronstadt, where the First Battle Cruiser was visiting.

On the cricket field Yorkshire had held out for a draw against Notts. Fred Bowley, who played for Worcestershire from 1899 to 1923, scoring over 20,000 runs, scored 276 against Hampshire at Dudley out of 474-6. The Royal Navy beat the Army and Eton and Winchester drew. Most significantly Middlesex and Surrey, the top two, now met at the Oval and Surrey scored 502-6 despite a rare failure from Hobbs. There were hundreds from Andrew Ducat, later an FA Cup Winner with Aston Villa, and Cyril Wilkinson, later an Olympic hockey gold medallist.

On 30 June *The Times* reported on a meeting of the House of Commons Channel Tunnel Committee. Lord Wolseley had been worrying about the hypothetical tunnel being used for invasion. Lord Sydenham thought it unlikely. Since the attempt to dig a tunnel had been abandoned in 1882 this all seemed a little fanciful.

The paper continued to deal with the assassination as a blow to the House of Hapsburg, but not as something that could mean anything at all to Britain. Much more problematical, of course, was the continuing danger of civil war in Ireland, and yet again the main editorial addressed itself to the subject. In a report on the state of the Ulster Volunteers *The Times* talks about gun running with no note of condemnation.

The parliamentary report opened by saying that a Labour member, Mr John Hodge, had entered the house wearing 'a very light brown summer suit and a brown straw trilby hat'. Despite this wild eccentricity he was not expelled. He was to volunteer for the Army but be rejected because of his age (he was 59). The main thrust of the day's debate was Persia and in particular Anglo-Persian Oil: now that the Royal Navy had many oil-burning ships, maintaining supplies was a matter of importance.

At the Oval, with a crowd of over 10,000 again, Surrey were out for 544 and Middlesex scored 267 in reply. *The Times* referred to 'plucky batting' though it is not entirely clear why as there is no suggestion that the wicket was in any way difficult. Mr C.O.H.Sewell, the South African-born captain of Gloucestershire, made 102 against Kent. At Dudley Worcestershire went on to 494 and Hampshire reached 362-7. The Hon A.E.Mulholland made 132 for the Household Brigade against the Green Jackets. Andrew Mulholland was to die at Ypres in November. Lionel Tennyson, having just played for The Army, turned out for the Green Jackets, his military duties mostly seeming to consist of playing cricket. Yorkshire failed again, bowled out for 150 by Essex at Leeds, Essex making 130-6 in reply. At Brighton Nottinghamshire scored 426-2 with Joe Hardstaff unbeaten on 180.

There was a letter in *The Times* warning about the white slave traffic: according to the writer, women dressed as nuns frequented continental ports and stations pretending that they were there to take care of young women travelling alone.

On the following day *The Times* proclaimed 'Middlesex still unbeaten'. J.W.Hearne had put his head down for 191* and at the close Middlesex were 393-5. The game between Worcestershire and Hampshire was also drawn. Hampshire were left to get 282 in 95 minutes, but did manage 147-0 in the time with J.Stone, top scorer in the first innings with 83, adding 100 not out. James Stone was another ageing professional who would not come back after the war.

The Hon Andrew Mulholland made another hundred in the second innings for the Household Brigade in his last appearance for which there is a record. Haverford College, having perhaps now got their land legs, comprehensively beat Uppingham.

June was over - nobody knew what fateful events had taken place.

Frank Tarrant

Sydney Smith

Colin Blythe

Percy Jeeves

Tom Hayward

Five players for whom the season of 1914 was their last in English first-class cricket. [Roger Mann Collection]

DERBYSHIRE 1914
Standing (l to r): A.J.Atfield (umpire), S.Cadman, A.Morton, J.Horsley,
H.Wild, G.Beet, A.G.Slater, J.Bowden, A.A.White (umpire).
Seated (l to r): J Chapman, T.Forester, R.R.C.Baggallay (capt),
G.Curgenven, L.Oliver. In front: H.G.Blacklidge (coach).
[Derbyshire CCC Photographic Archive]

GLOUCESTERSHIRE 1914
Standing (l to r): H.Smith, T.Langdon, T.H.Gange, E.G.Dennett,
A.E.Dipper, F.E.Ellis. Seated (l to r): W.S.Grant, M.A.Green,
C.O.H.Sewell (capt.). T.Miller, C.W.L.Parker.
This is the side which played Sussex at Hastings on 13, 14 and 15 July 1914.
[Gloucestershire CCC]

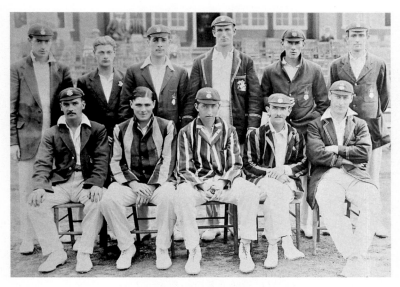

HAMPSHIRE 1914
Standing (l to r): W.H.Livsey, J.H.Down, A.S.Kennedy, G.Brown,
H.A.W.Bowell, J.A.Newman. Seated (l to r): J.Stone, H.A.H. Smith,
A.Jaques (capt.),J.G.Greig, C.P.Mead.
[Hampshire CCC]

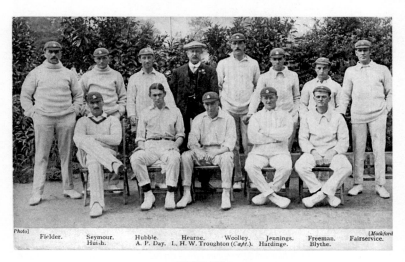

KENT 1914
[Kent CCC]

LEICESTERSHIRE 1914
Standing (l to r): S.C.Packer (Secretary), W.Shipman, G.Geary, A.Skelding,
W.E.Astill, H.Whitehead, T.E.Sidwell, S.Coe. Seated (l to r): J.H.King, A.T.Sharp,
J.Shields, C.J.B.Wood (capt.), W.N.Riley, H.Wright, T.Burdett.
[Leicestershire CCC]

NORTHAMPTONSHIRE 1914
Standing (l to r): W.East, W.Wells, C.N.Woolley, G.J.Thompson, W.A.Buswell,
L Bullimer (scorer), F.I.Walden. Seated (l to r): A.D.Denton, W.H.Denton,
S.G.Smith (capt.), J.S.Denton, R.A.Haywood
This is the side which played Sussex at Hove on 30, 31 July and 1 August 1914.
The Dentons are wearing their Wellingborough School blazers.
[John Watson Collection]

NOTTINGHAMSHIRE 1914
Standing (l to r): F.G.Roberts (umpire), H.Coxon (scorer), T.G.Wass,
F.Barratt, W.R.D.Payton, G.M.Lee, M.Robinson (reporter), R.G.Barlow (umpire),.
Seated (l to r): J.R.Gunn, J.Iremonger, P.J.S.Pearson-Gregory (capt),
G.Gunn, T.W.Oates. On ground (l to r); W.Walker, J.Hardstaff snr, W.W.Whysall.
This was the side which played against Sussex at Hove
on 29, 30 June and 1 July 1914.
[Nottinghamshire CCC]

SOMERSET 1914
Standing (l to r): W.Hyman, A.D.E.Rippon, E.Robson, J.J.Bridges,
A.G.Marshall, H.Chidgey. Seated (l to r): P.P.Hope, B.D.Hylton-Stewart,
E.S.M.Poyntz (capt.), L.C.Braund, E.C.Ball
This is team which played Sussex at Hove on 6, 7 July 1914.

SURREY 1914
Champion County
[Surrey CCC]

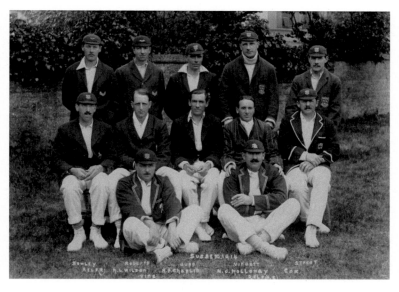

SUSSEX 1914
Standing (l to r): E.H.Bowley, H.E.Roberts, V.W.C.Jupp, J.H.Vincett, G.B.Street.
Seated (l to r): R.R.Relf, H.L.Wilson, H.P.Chaplin (capt.), N.J.Holloway, G.R.Cox
On ground (l to r): J Vine, A.E.Relf.
[Sussex Cricket Museum]

WARWICKSHIRE 1914
Standing (l to r): C.S.Baker, C.Charlesworth, S.Santall, J.H.Parsons,
E.F.Field, P.Jeeves. Seated (l to r): S.Kinneir, W.G.Quaife,
F.R.Foster (capt.), E.B.Crockford, E.J.Smith.
This is the side which played Leicestershire at Edgbaston on
18, 19 and 20 May 1914.
[Warwickshire CCC]

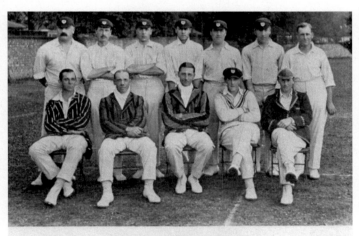

1914.
.. D. Burrows, F. L. Bowley, C. G. A. Collier, F. Chester, A. J. Conway, E. Bale, F. Pearso
J. A. Cuffe, A. T. Cliff. W. H. Taylor (Capt.), M. K. Foster, G. N. Foster.

WORCESTERSHIRE
[Worcestershire CCC]

G. Bayes   B. B. Wilson   P. Holmes   M. W. Booth   T. Birtles   A. Drake   J. Hoyland
(Scorer)

YORKSHIRE COUNTY CRICKET TEAM.—1914.

A. Dolphin   S. Haigh   D. Denton   Sir A. W. White, Bt.   G. H. Hirst   W. Rhodes   R. Kilner
(Captain)

THE LAST YORKSHIRE XI. PHOTOGRAPH

[Brian Sanderson/YCCC Archives]

HURSTPIERPOINT COLLEGE 1st XI 1914
Standing (l to r): R.Lee, E.L.Pitcher, A.Goodger, M.A.Pitcher.
Seated (l to r): C.T.Stuart, R.F.Crux, D.R.Baylis (capt.), R.Lintott, M.C.Nicholson.
On ground (l to r): G.W.E.Baker, L.H.R.E.Flindt
Stuart, Lintott and Flindt were killed in action, Bayliss married the Headmaster's
daughter and M.A.Pitcher founded the Old Hurst Johnian Cricket Week in 1920.
[Hurstpierpoint College Archives]

1ST XI CRICKET.

H.K CASSELS.   E C CUNNINGHAM.   A L. KEMP Esq.   C.E. CHANNING.   V. G. PARSONS.
C W. SHORT.   B G. WHITFIELD.   R. C. S. BROWNE (capt)   H.V.A.CORFIELD.   O. E. J. McOUSTRA.
J. E. PRIDHAM.

ST. LAWRENCE COLLEGE 1st XI.
Corfield, Parsons and Beaumont were killed in action.
Cassels was later an Olympic hockey player.
[St Lawrence College]

NEATH CRICKET CLUB 2nd XI 1914
A thoughtful looking group with a number of young players present,
probably taken towards the end of the season.
[Glamorgan CCC]

ESSEX v WORCESTERSHIRE
Colchester Festival 18, 19 and 20 June 1914
Back row (l to r): W.Reeves, ?, C.D.McIver, F.L.Bowley, F.Chester, ?, A.F.Lane,
F.A.Pearson, ? Standing (l to r): Umpire, ?, C.A.G.Russell, G.B.Davies,
W.M.F.Turner (?), R.D.Burrows, C.G.A.Collier, E.W.Bale, B.Tremlin, ?, ?, ?,
Umpire. Seated (l to r): F.L.Fane, F.H.Gillingham, P.A.Perrin, J.W.H.T.Douglas,
H.D.Swan, W.H.Taylor, M.K.Foster, A.T.Cliff, B.G.Stevens
On ground(l to r): H.A.Carpenter ?, ?, ?
The umpires were TA Brown and WAJ West.
[Worcestershire CCC]

ST PAUL'S SCHOOL 1ST XI 1914
Standing (l to r): Kerry (pro), Hyne (pro), D.J.Hamilton, R.G.Seale, W.A Rob-
erts, G.M.Baker, J Carlin (pro). Seated (l to r): E.G.J.Gibb, A.J.W.Pearson,
C.H.L.Skeet (capt), M.L.Hayne, J.Rayner. On ground (l to r): J.L.F.Hunt,
C.J.Sharp.
Pearson, Rayne and Roberts were killed in action. Skeet was an Oxford blue
who also played for Middlesex.

Chapter Six

July 1914

On 1 July Mr N.E.Brookes defeated Herr Froitzheim in the final round of the gentlemen's singles at Wimbledon; however the contest was still played on a challenge basis, so Norman Brookes of Australia had to challenge Anthony Wilding of New Zealand, who had held the title for the previous four years. Wilding (who had played first-class cricket for Canterbury) was to be another casualty of the war, dying at Neuve Chapelle in May 1915.

The Archbishop of Sarajevo, Dr Stadler, was reported to have said that 'the crime was a consequence of historical development, and that it must have taken place sooner or later', a somewhat gnomic utterance, as it seems unlikely that the Archbishop of Sarajevo was a Marxist. All manner of conspiracy theories were emerging, although Princip himself claimed at this point to have been acting alone.

Ireland remained the chief political problem. The House of Lords was still debating the amending bill which was intended to go some way to allay the suspicions of Ulster by temporarily excluding the six counties of Ulster (something of a forlorn hope).

In the County Championship, Surrey went to Northampton and were bowled out for 177, though Northants were 8 for 2 at the close.

Frank Tarrant, somewhat surprisingly, turned out for MCC and Ground against Eton in a one-day game, taking four wickets and making 36 not out (Middlesex had no game that day), though the main contributor was William Tod, a former Eton captain, who made an unbeaten 94.

There was huge scoring at Brighton where the game ended with Notts 501-3 declared and 198-3 (George Gunn 104*) and Sussex 499. H.P.Chaplin scored 213* for Sussex. Chaplin was the Sussex captain and this was his highest first-class score. He was an Old Harrovian, but his early first-class cricket had been in India. This kind of scoring rather made the case for amending the LBW law and there was a letter in *The Times* from Mr Robert Lyttleton urging such a change.

For Kent against Gloucestershire Frank Woolley scored 77 and 111 not out as well as taking twelve for 122. In this match he outbowled Blythe who bowled 32 overs without taking a wicket.

Lancashire, on the very brink of defeat against Warwickshire, were saved by the rain – they were 100-9 having been set 295. As Lancashire had led on first innings, they took three points from the game to Warwickshire's one.

The *Manchester Guardian* carried a score in the Mayo-Robson Challenge Cup, a game between Liverpool and Manchester Universities: but Leeds won the trophy (which appears to have been played between these three). You would not have known from anything in the London press that there were other universities than Oxford and Cambridge.

On 2 July the Northants v Surrey game remained poised. In a low-scoring match Northants needed 154 to win after S.G.Smith took five for 12. At the close they were 17-2.

At Hull Hampshire managed to bowl Yorkshire out for 152 but were themselves 34-3 at the close, having lost all three to Alonzo Drake.

It was Speech Day at Harrow with the Headmaster's comments reported at length by *The Times*: most of it a complaint that the universities expected some knowledge of Greek for those who were to read Classics, saying that this meant those boys had to be 'crammed' for the entrance exams.

The article headed 'Day of British defeats' turned out on this occasion to refer to Henley and Wimbledon. At Henley 'on every side one heard French and German and American spoken'.

On Monday 6 July there was a small item to say that the Army had decided to allow certain reservists to return to the colours to complete their engagements: they had to be unmarried and would return with the rank of Private. Note that there is no pressure here, no suggestion that they are actually needed.

As far as cricket was concerned, this was the first day of the University match and *The Times* went through the prospects in some detail on the news pages as well as on the sports pages. In the Championship Middlesex gained some ground by beating Worcestershire by an innings despite the loss of the second day's play to rain. Tarrant (110) and J.W.Hearne (103*) were, as usual, the main exponents as the county went from 80-3 to 314-6 declared at some considerable speed, then both took wickets as Worcestershire were bowled out for 114, losing with ninety minutes to spare.

On the same day there was a long report in the *Daily Mirror* on the AAA Championships at Stamford Bridge: there were only summarised cricket scores. A small headline said,' Fine batting by G.O.Gauld' (note that the *Mirror* did not add "Mr"). Gauld had made 90 (his career best) for Nottinghamshire against Derbyshire. An occasional player, he was captaining the county as A.O.Jones was ill. There were pictures from the tennis final at Wimbledon (which also got a write-up) and of the pole vault from the AAA Championships. The editorial talked about Joseph Chamberlain (and the pictures on the front page were of his funeral). The paper does mention that the Commons was 'on the edge of a storm over Ireland.'

The following day – Tuesday 7 – was a Joseph Chamberlain funeral special for the *Daily Mirror*. 'Umbrella forest at cricket match,' it said, reporting on Oxford v Cambridge. There was a brief description of the day's play and full scores for this and county matches (amateurs had initials, of course). What the *Mirror* did have (as did all of the cheaper papers and many local ones) was a romantic serial which kept running when other things were squeezed. The *Daily Mirror's* favourite author was Ruby M.Ayres. At this point she only wrote for serialisation, with her first novel (of 150) not published until 1916. Later, the *Dictionary of National Biography* called her '"one of the most popular and prolific romantic novelists of the twentieth century"'.

Surrey, starting a game against Lancashire at Old Trafford, reached 371-5, Ernie Hayes being top scorer with 102*. The loss of time to rain allowed Hampshire to get away with a draw against Yorkshire, with scores of 103 and 79-7 hardly showing the batting to advantage.

Oxford's last warm-up match was against Mr Lionel Robinson's XI at Old Buckenham Hall in Norfolk., where their bowling was thumped by Sir Timothy O'Brien who made 90 and 111 in his last first-class match (and his first since 1907) at the age of 51. Not bad for a man who had made his first-class debut in 1881.

On 7 July there was a report of a strike at the Royal Arsenal at Woolwich, with a threat to call out men at the dockyards. An engineer called Entwistle had been dismissed after refusing to erect machinery on concrete poured out by a non-unionist.

The Vienna correspondent of *The Times* reported that 'reflection is prompting a more moderate tone in the Austro-Hungarian discussion of the hypothetical complicity of Servia in the Sarajevo crime.' Nothing to worry about, then.

In the cricket reports, of course, the University match took pride of place. 5,710 people paid to enter and the paper estimated that there were about 9,000 people there by tea-time. Oxford batted first and were out for 239. The only man scoring over 30 was the wicketkeeper, E.A.Shaw, who batted at No.9, making an undefeated 57.It was his highest score in his last first-class innings: he died on the Somme in 1916. In reply Cambridge had made 40 without loss.

The teams had been announced for Gentlemen v Players, both at Lord's and immediately afterwards at the Oval.

Hampshire were all for 134 at Birmingham, F.R.Foster taking six for 63. He then made 75 as Warwickshire reached 217-8 at the close. At Old Trafford Surrey closed on 393 and dismissed Lancashire for 216, 'Razor' Smith taking five wickets. Smith had a reputation for being deadly on soft wickets but very prone to injury and illness. In the damp summer of 1910 he had taken 247 wickets. He did not reappear after the war, his body no longer up to the strain, and he went to work for Stuart Surridge, the bat-makers. Lancashire followed on and made 43-0 at the second attempt so Surrey sat in a strong position after two days.

At Sheffield Yorkshire were out for 101 against Kent of which Roy Kilner made 50: Kent were 96-5. At Brighton Somerset were dismissed for 68 (the previous match at Brighton had produced 1198 runs and only 16 wickets). 40 of the 68 came from Len Braund and A.E.Relf took 6-27: the six amateur batsmen in the side managed 17 between them. By the close Sussex were 269-8.

The Household Brigade, who seemed to have nothing much to do but play cricket, were playing the Eton Ramblers.

The Times swimming club held an 88-yard handicap at the Lambeth Baths: obviously swimming pools were then built to the length of a cricket pitch.

On the following day (in the papers on 8 July) it was reported that two Russian tramps had been arrested near Beaumont sur Oise: they spoke no French, carried no money, but were apparently carrying home-made bombs and said that they were anarchists and intended to assassinate the Tsar on his forthcoming visit to France. It seemed at least possible that they were actually members of the Tsar's secret police.

The Woolwich Arsenal strike had ended with an agreement to set up a court of enquiry into the cause.

In the University Match Cambridge were out for 225 despite many dropped catches and *The Times* was critical of batsmen stepping in front of the wicket and padding the ball away, which was not quite the thing in such distinguished company. At the second attempt Oxford were 168-5. *The Times* suggested that Mr Bristowe 'is the only class bowler on either side'.

Surrey beat Lancashire by an innings with five more wickets for "Razor" Smith. Sussex beat Somerset without much difficulty and Warwickshire only failed to beat Hampshire because it rained. Philip Mead had made 115 but, as so often, had little support. Worcestershire's later batsmen scored heavily against Gloucestershire to take their total to 406 and a lead of 235. R.D.Burrows, batting at No.10, made 107 not out: he was 43 years old and did reappear in 1919, but not beyond that. In a low-scoring match Kent beat Yorkshire at Bramall Lane, with Colin Blythe taking eight for 55 and Kent then making heavy weather of getting 77, losing five wickets for 40 and relying on the batting of "Punter" Humphreys who made 40 not out.

The Times reported on a British naval visit to Kiel at which a good time was had by all. The paper was taking a relaxed view of Germany's increasing naval strength. There was some mention of Sarajevo, mostly concerning the extent to which it was sheer bad luck.

The University Match ended on 8 July in a victory for Oxford by 194 runs, Cambridge collapsing for 73 after it rained. *The Times* produced the University averages for the season. Oxford's batting was topped by Donald Knight (enough to make him one of *Wisden's* five for 1915) who played for some years after the war for Surrey though mainly in the school holidays. He later wrote two books on cricket, *The Compleat Cricketer* and The *More Compleat Cricketer*.

Amongst those who also batted is R.T.Stanyforth who played two innings in the season for eight runs (he played the one match against MCC). He continued to play Army cricket after the war then captained England's tour of South Africa in 1927/28 without having played county cricket. He had three games for Yorkshire in 1928 and then went to the West Indies with MCC in 1929/30 as vice-captain, but did not play in the Tests. In 1935 he published a book called *Wicketkeeping* and during the Second World War was GSO1 of the 21st Army Group. He toured with various private teams in Egypt and Canada and is last seen captaining the Lord Mayor of Newcastle's XI in a one-day game at Jesmond in 1944 at the age of 52.

On Friday 10 July there was word that the Representative Church Council had decided to give women the right to vote for and sit on parochial council – perhaps the very thin end of the wedge that led to women bishops one hundred years later.

The Times' first leader, as every day for some weeks now, was about Ireland.

The Eton and Harrow match began at Lord's. This was analysed as closely as the University match and took the headlines despite the start of the Gentlemen v Players match at the Oval. The Oval game was regarded as small beer by *The Times*, the score coming after the county matches (and Oxford University Authentics against the Household Brigade and Haileybury v Haverford).

Somerset were out for 115 against Kent, with the only resistance coming from the captain, Mr E.S.M.Poyntz, who made 51*. The 1911 census shows Poyntz (then 28) as a hop merchant. He had played for Somerset for a few years and was appointed captain for 1913. A career average for the county of 16.07 and a highest score of 89 suggests a rather average amateur batsman – he did make 114 in 70 minutes for The Army against Cambridge University in 1919, when he also played a last couple of games for Somerset.

Against Hampshire at Bristol, Gloucestershire were bowled out by Kennedy and Newman for 34. Hampshire made 216 with a century from Mead and Gloucestershire were 27-0 in their second innings. Cecil Parkin, at this point (like James Tyldesley) playing for Lancashire only when not required by his league club Church, had taken thirteen wickets as Leicestershire ended the second day with nine second-innings down and 17 runs ahead.

The next report shows the London Clergy fairly beating up the Southwark Clergy in a one-day match (London 340-8, Southwark 105 and 82-8). The Rev'd R Sheppard who kept wicket for London was almost certainly Dick Sheppard, later known for founding the Peace Pledge Union.

At the Oval the Players made 321, thanks to a last-wicket stand of 122 between Hitch and Strudwick after Hobbs, Tarrant and J.W.Hearne – the form men of the summer – were all out with only 12 scored. Two of them fell to Ernest Kirk, a somewhat surprising selection since at this point he had played only two games for Surrey, in one of which he had bowled only five overs: still it was at the Oval and he may have been a late selection. *The Times* muttered about Jaques bowling leg theory with only one man on the off side.

On 11 July it was reported that Sir Edward Carson was off to Belfast to foment trouble by addressing the "Ulster provisional government". The extent to which *The Times* sided with the unionists as they edged closer and closer to rebellion is remarkable. Winston Churchill, speaking in Dundee, said that he was confident that British good sense would prevail. Very few commentators at the time would have credited Churchill, impulsive and warlike, with that particular virtue.

The Eton v Harrow match got an article to itself in the news pages rather than just among the other scores. Harrow made 232, Eton 146. *The Times* goes on to list the spectators in the carriages and the more distinguished ones in the stands as if it were royal ball rather than a cricket match. There were no anarchists here.

The other cricket reports led with Gentlemen v Players. The Gentlemen were 90 behind on first innings, being out for 237 with the Players 143-3 in their second innings; they were slow but then Arthur Jaques was bowling his leg theory again. Keeping wicket for the Gentlemen was Harold Garnett of Lancashire. By the end of the season he was opening the batting, keeping wicket and captaining Lancashire all at once. He died at Cambrai in December 1917.

At Huddersfield Northamptonshire were bowled out twice in a day for 146 and 192 to leave Yorkshire winning by an innings. Kent beat Somerset by nine wickets: Lancashire beat Leicestershire by eight wickets, the report headed 'Lancashire's new bowler' with reference to Cecil Parkin who took 14 for 99 in the match. Parkin had played one match for Yorkshire in 1906, but this was his debut for Lancashire at the age of 28.

In 1906 Parkin had told Lord Hawke on the morning of his Yorkshire debut that he had actually (just) been born in Durham, to which the noble lord replied, 'We are not particular about a few yards; you play today'[26] A telegram from MCC lodging an objection to qualification followed. Parkin joined Tunstall in the North Staffordshire League, later moving to Church in the Lancashire League and subsequently Rochdale which meant that he only played for Lancashire when free. Gloucestershire were not quite so bad in their second innings against Hampshire: Kennedy and Newman took ten wickets apiece in the match.

On 13 July *The Times* had three leaders, dealing with Ulster, the death of Lady Hardinge and the report into the loss of the *Empress of Ireland.* It reported the sudden death of M Hartwig, the Russian Minister at Belgrade – he had a sudden fatal heart attack while in conversation with his opposite number from Vienna. It was not in itself a crucial point, but it emphasised the rising unrest in the Balkans. *The Times* reported on 'panic' among Austrians in Belgrade who believed they were to be murdered in their beds. The Austrian government was said to believe that two Russian anarchists had arrived in Belgrade (complete with bombs) to blow up the

26   Cecil Parkin, *Cricket Triumphs and Troubles*, Nicholls & Co, 1936

Austrian legation. 'The occurrence,' said *The Times* weightily, 'is likely to assist admirably those persons on both sides of the frontier whose desire, to judge by the utterances of a certain section of the Austro-Hungarian and Servian press, seems to be to prevent the tranquillization of public opinion in either country.' Which seems to be taking things rather lightly.

The crucial question was the extent of official Serbian involvement with the assassin. It appeared probable that there was no top-level involvement though members of the Serbian armed forces had helped the assassins with their training and had helped them get into the country. It was all helping to strengthen the "war party" in Austria-Hungary (the Hungarian end of the dual monarchy being much less keen on war). Austria was preparing the ultimatum for Serbia (hampered by the fact that a large part of the Austrian army had gone off on the traditional "harvest leave".

Some historians suggest that France and Britain were unreasonably nonchalant about the prospects of war (and *The Times* certainly was); but two recent Balkan wars had been contained so why should this be any different? The answer to that for the moment was that Germany was supportive of any move by Austria to go to war against Serbia. Germany calculated that Russia would not get involved on Serbia's behalf, and that England most certainly would not want to get into the action.

There was a report from St Petersburg that an 'unknown woman' had fatally stabbed Rasputin (described by *The Times* as a 'peasant fakir'). The news had been exaggerated: Rasputin had indeed been stabbed but he would recover.

The Eton v Harrow match turned round with Harrow out for 146 in their second innings (R.A.C.Foster, later wounded when a Lieutenant in the Rifle Brigade, but who lived until 1916, taking four for 16) and Eton making 233-6, *The Times* singling out C.J.Hambro as a potential great batsman. Charles Hambro (of the banking family), though appearing in many minor matches for everyone from the Eton Ramblers to the Butterflies, never, in fact, played first-class cricket. He turned out for the Household Brigade against the Public Schools in August 1916 just before being sent out to the Western Front with the Coldstream Guards where he won the Military Cross. His last recorded game was for the Bank of England Governor's XI against the Bank of England in 1931.

There was an active day at Coalville where Worcestershire scored 223 (Frank Chester 93) and Leicestershire 174-3 of which Harry Whitehead made 103. Derbyshire made 431-8 against Lancashire (no Parkin this time).

The Times saw the team selection for Gentlemen v Players at Lord's as more important than the result of the game at the Oval. There Hobbs made 156 and Percy Jeeves took four for 41, 'No bowler of today,' said *The Times*, 'achieves such speed with so little effort as Jeeves' and it thought that he would very likely be successful in Australia. It was not to be: he was to die in action in 1916, though his surname was immortalised by P.G.Wodehouse.

In Ulster 12 July had been celebrated with even more than usual enthusiasm. 70,000 Orangemen had marched from Belfast to Drumbeg. *The Times* leader 'Dallying with Danger' was of course about Ireland. The fleet was being mobilised by Churchill, crews being brought up to strength. There was a dock strike on the Mersey.

A piece in *The Times* talked about 'three kinds of cricket match' at Lord's, saying that,

> The University match is one-half cricket and one-half society. At the Eton and Harrow match many more of the spectators go to see the frocks than the game. At the Gentlemen v Players it is all stern cricket and nothing else.

On the first day of that match the Gentlemen had been dismissed for 265 which was a substantial recovery after Barnes and Hitch had reduced them to 37 for 4. As these two were supported by Tarrant, Kennedy and J.W.Hearne the Players had a formidable attack. Only S.G.Smith, described by *The Times* as 'at the moment perhaps the best amateur batsman in England,' reached 50. By the close the Players were 58-2.

At Tunbridge Wells Essex were bowled out by Fielder and Blythe for 138 and by the close Kent had rampaged to 303-3, Seymour 139* in 165 minutes. If James Seymour is now best remembered as the man who would take the Inland Revenue to court and win, he scored well over 25,000 runs for Kent during a lengthy career, with 53 centuries to his name.

J.H.King made 227* against Worcestershire at Coalville. John King was already 43 and this was his highest county score, but he carried on for Leicestershire until 1925, when he was 54. 25,122 first-class runs and 1,204 wickets was a fair haul in a career which spread over thirty years.

Derbyshire carried on to 504 against Lancashire with a last-wicket stand of 93 by Numbers ten and eleven, J. Humphries and J. Horsley: Lancashire were all out for 204 in reply.

The Times also carried the score for the Green Jackets against I Zingari. The inexhaustible Teddy Wynyard turned out for I Zingari in pursuit of yet another century for his scrapbook, but this time he only made 73.

On 15 July, though 'all was quiet in Belfast,' Ireland remained the obsession. It was reported that Rasputin was still alive after all. There was anxiety about Albania but nothing else about the Balkans.

A special article on Tunbridge Wells concentrated on the social side, lamenting from that point of view that Kent had wrapped up their game against Essex in two days. Seymour had gone on to 214 and W.J.Fairservice then bowled Essex out again. Bill Fairservice played for Kent from 1902 until 1921, then put in a few years for Northumberland.

There was a new pavilion to replace the one burned down earlier in the year: the town was full of bunting and coloured lights. There was a full social programme and the band played during the cricket. There had been two performances of Robert Marshall's *The Duke of Killiecrankie* at the

Opera House. And there was cricket as well.

Meanwhile at Lord's the Players were bowled out for 256 by J.W.H.T.Douglas who took a remarkable nine for 105. The Gentlemen were 148-2 at the second attempt in a game which at this stage looked fairly even. *The Times* correspondent complained that modern players used heavy bats and so restricted their wristwork.

Lancashire saved the game at Derby with J.T.Tyldesley making 98. Apart from Johnny Tyldesley, Lancashire included his brother Ernest and an unrelated pair William and Harry whose third brother James did not play in this match. Dick – yet another brother – would make his debut in 1919.

Leicestershire beat Worcestershire by an innings at Coalville, with George Geary taking eleven wickets in the match. Geary had just turned 21 and was by this season a fixture in the XI, as he would be until 1938. At Hastings Gloucestershire, needing over 400 to win, were a dismal 12-3. A.E.Relf had made 121 in 105 minutes as Sussex raced to 368-8 before declaring in their second innings. Albert Relf was 40 but would reappear for a couple of years after the war.

On 16 July the 'foreign affairs' summary in *The Times* is neat enough. France worried about military deficiencies (as opposed to Germany): a Russian reply to a Persian memorandum; skirmishes in Albania and a meeting between the Grand Vizier and Venizelos, the Greek Prime Minister. Nothing there that is the stuff of immediate crisis.

That day, though, *The Times* had an editorial on Austria-Hungary and Servia which dismissed recent events as a panic but worried about the effects of noise being made in the press on both sides, and especially the 'reckless and provocative' behaviour of Serbian newspapers. *The Times* remained confident that the Emperor and his most sagacious advisers would continue to act with self-possession. There was just a hint of 'a peril to European peace.'

At Lord's heavy overnight rain had affected the pitch. The Gentlemen went on to 275 without anyone scoring heavily, and then the top of the Players' batting collapsed utterly to 28-6 before being all out for 150 and losing by 134 runs. Douglas (13 wickets in the match) took four for 67 and Frank Foster four for 56. *The Times* was displeased, saying that 'the failure of England's best professional batsmen to play fast bowling such as that of Mr Douglas and Mr Foster would be comic if it were not pathetic.' It blamed this on the modern style of batting, of trying to move your feet rather than lunge forwards. It seems to be the usual problem of sporting journalism of trying to derive some universal truth from a single performance.

Sussex finished off Gloucestershire with ease, N.J.Holloway and J.H.Vincett bowling them out for 75 for a 364 run win.

A Mr C.D.Williams wrote to the newspapers proposing the establishment of a fund to get for Harrow 'an absolutely first-class coach' in a slightly alarmist reaction to their having lost this year's game to Eton: he intended to raise the money from Old Harrovians in the City.

On 17 July the piece on Count Tisza's speech in the Austro-Hungarian parliament had as a sub-heading 'War as a last resort', which was more or less Tisza's view – he was at the most cautious end of the Empire's response. It suggested that yesterday's leader was being seen in some quarters as 'an English warning to Servia' and the assumption seemed to be that having seen this in *The Times* the Serbs would come to their senses (though the reports of riot and rampage in Belgrade which appeared in some of the Austrian papers were groundless).

Georges Carpentier of France defeated Gunboat Smith of the USA at Olympia for the 'white heavyweight championship of the world'. The shadow of Jack Johnson loomed large.

At Tunbridge Wells the wicket was doubtful after rain and Nottinghamshire (captained this time by Arthur Carr) were all out for 137 against Blythe and Woolley. By the close Kent were 100-6. A.P.Day, on 38 not out, was the day's highest scorer. Arthur Day was an amateur and two of his brothers also played for the county (and both also played football for the Corinthians).

From the championship point of view it was the return of Middlesex (who had cunningly rested through the two Gentlemen v Players matches) that was of the most interest. They dismissed Essex for 168 at Lord's (Hearne and Tarrant as usual) and then reached 137-5 with J.W.Hearne unbeaten on 55. There were fourteen amateurs playing: Essex's crop of eight being far less distinguished than Middlesex's six.

There were more concerned letters about the state of cricket at Harrow, offering various remedies.

On 18 July the papers reported that the setting up of a national council on venereal disease had been announced. The King was off to spend the weekend with the Fleet at Spithead. The cabinet had met twice to discuss Ireland and try to find a way forward. There was the usual whining on all sides following the Carpentier/Smith fight.

At Tunbridge Wells Kent gained a first-innings lead of 33 as Blythe and Woolley bowled Nottinghamshire out again for 195, but Kent's smallish target of 163 looked a long way off as they were 20-3 by the close.

At Lord's Middlesex had worked their way into a good position. They had reached 329 with runs down the order. There was 51 from Patsy Hendren, batting at No.7. In 1914 Hendren was an unremarkable county player, though he had first played in 1907. It would be very different after the war. The lead was 161: at the close Essex were 206-5 with mainly unreliable amateurs left to bat.

Hampshire had beaten Worcestershire – from an overnight 136-9 Jaques and Livsey had added 107 for the last wicket, so gaining a lead of 88. Jaques and Kennedy bowled out Worcestershire for 179 and Hampshire won by 8 wickets.

An 'Old Harrow captain' wrote to say that the school had been spending

£300 a year on professional bowlers. There was a long report on the amateur epee championship, referring to France as a county where 'swordplay is still the national game'. Central Europe went unmentioned.

On 20 July the main item of news was that the King had called the various parties together to try to solve the Irish situation – he had cancelled his visit to the Fleet.

The Scottish miners had asked the Miners' Federation of Great Britain to ballot at its conference on the question of a general stoppage in their support. The Scottish miners were on strike because the employers were proposing a reduction in wages.

J.H.Thomas (Jimmy Thomas, then Labour MP for Derby), speaking in Darlington, suggested that if army officers were prepared to plead conscience to rebel (over the Irish question) then the working class should be permitted to say that troops should not interfere in industrial disputes.

It was being proposed to hold a conference of clergymen's wives and women church workers to discuss the ordination of women as priests in the Church of England. *The Times* felt (correctly) that it would get no support from the Church in general.

The rhetoric was being wound up here and there in Austria and Serbia, with the notion of 'greater Servia' being floated. The real political activity was not noticed. President Poincare of France had arrived in Kronstadt on a visit to Russia – the thought of France and Russia being able to communicate easily was making Austria and Germany nervous.

At Chesterfield Yorkshire demolished Derbyshire by an innings. Derbyshire's second innings score was 68 of which Arthur Morton made 50. At one time Derbyshire were 64-2 but Alonzo Drake took five for 6 in three overs, including four wickets in four balls (four amateurs of no great merit, to be sure). It was Drake's last year of first-class cricket, though he played a few games in the Bradford League during the war. He was not a well man, declared unfit for military service, and he died early in 1919.

Kent failed to reach their target at Tunbridge Wells as Nottinghamshire won by 32 runs with Joe Iremonger taking six for 39 to follow his seven for 61 in the first innings. 1914 was Iremonger's last season in first-class cricket. He remained in the game after the war, being Nottinghamshire coach from 1921 to 1938.

At Northampton the game was drawn, but Walter Buswell, the Northamptonshire wicketkeeper, who had batted at No.11 in the first innings, was sent up the order and made 101*, his only first-class hundred.

Middlesex concluded a fairly easy victory against Essex, so staying at the top of the Championship table. Surrey and Lancashire had started on Saturday, Surrey scoring 401, which included Hobbs' sixth century of the season (he made 142). *The Times* remarked on the absence of Parkin.

In the first–class averages, unusually enough, the first five in the batting were professionals (Hearne, Mead, Tarrant, Hardstaff and Hobbs) while three of the first five in the bowling were amateurs (S.G.Smith, Jaques and Geoffrey Davies of Essex and Cambridge University). Alec Kennedy had become the first to reach 100 wickets for the season, helping to keep Hampshire as high as fourth.

On 21 July the exciting news was that the trial of Mme Caillaux had begun in Paris. Wife of the former Prime Minister, she was giving her evidence. Feeling her husband traduced and slandered by *Le Figaro*, she had taken matters into her own hands, made an appointment with M Calmette, the editor, and shot him dead. Over the next week or so, the trial was to occupy far more minds in Europe than the prospect of war.

For the *Daily Express* the front page was about the palace conference on Ireland, with a second feature on Mme Caillaux.

The *Express* provided a list of footballers who had been reinstated as amateurs by the FA (and those who had been refused). There was a fair amount of football chat (QPR moving to Shepherds Bush). As well as full scores and reports of county cricket, there was a column of club scores from the Home Counties and an announcement of the Cyphers Club week at Beckenham. B.D.Hylton-Stewart's 'breezy' hundred for Somerset against Essex was reported. He had, it said, 'been out of form recently, but in a county where talent is not abundant, he has been given a chance of finding it.' The sub head was 'Giving it Wood'. Hylton-Stewart had been to Bath College and in 1911 was living with his parents at Bath Rectory: his occupation shown as 'university student Cambridge'. He played three games for the university (though not winning a blue) but a fair few games for Somerset from 1912 to 1914. After the war he played minor county cricket for Hertfordshire.

The crisis in central Europe was beginning to seem worrying, with the impression that Austria was leaning hard on Serbia to make concessions (having in fact sent a note with which Serbia was most unlikely to comply) Share prices on the Vienna bourse had fallen heavily. And there were worries in Berlin.

Lancashire subsided completely at the Oval, bowled out twice in the day for 108 and 136 to lose by an innings and 158. At Southampton it was Alec Bowell's benefit and Sussex were all out for 196, Hampshire replying with 87-2. At Headingley, Yorkshire were bowled out for 75, James Iremonger taking six for 28 and Nottinghamshire were 136-7 in reply. At Maidstone Kent made 251 and Gloucestershire 108-8. Francis Ellis, in his first season for Gloucestershire, took six for 90.

The rumbling about coaching at Harrow continued, with a letter urging that something be heard from A.C.MacLaren.

The following day – 22 July – it was reported that a provisional agreement had been reached to install the Marconi wireless telegraphy system in ships. President Poincare's visit to St Petersburg was being disrupted by labour troubles. The Shah had been crowned and M Caillaux was giving evidence at his wife's trial.

The question of the demands made on Serbia by Austria-Hungary was becoming larger: the dual monarchy was reported to believe that it had the support of Germany and indeed England, while it expected Russia to hold back. The *Frankfurter Zeitung* is quoted as saying that no attempt should be made to secure from public opinion a blank power of attorney in support of the Vienna government, especially as the wisdom of Viennese policy is by no means above suspicion. Nowhere was there unconditional enthusiasm.

The conference on Ireland at Buckingham Palace had opened with a speech by the King.

The stock market in London was beginning to get nervous and falling at bad news from Central Europe.

At Headingley Yorkshire were pulling the game round: after a first-innings deficit of 86 they made 286 in their second innings. Alonzo Drake made 80 but there was controversy when he hit a return catch to Iremonger who tried to take the catch and throw the ball up in celebration, only for the umpire to decide that it had not been held long enough, and the game only continued after protests by the Nottinghamshire players and barracking from the crowd.

J.W.H.T.Douglas made 118 ('very slowly, as usual') and then took four for 30 against Somerset.

The Times gave MCC matches (certainly those played at Lord's) as much attention as county games and on this occasion the club beat the Royal Artillery by six wickets, though there was resistance from Mr R.H.Allen who made 112 and Captain W.W.Jelf, 77. Both carried on playing for the RA after the war. Born in Halifax, Nova Scotia, Wilfrid Jelf had played six games for Leicestershire in 1911: he managed only six runs in six innings and did not bowl.

In the *Daily Express* the Caillaux trial got rather more front-page room than the King's conference. Furthermore an American anarchist (a young woman) had gone on hunger strike and was to be tempted with chocolate, a technique apparently successful with wayward girls. J.W.H.T.Douglas was described as 'the Essex batting machine'. The listed fixtures include a number of club matches (this on a Wednesday).

On 23 July, 130,000 workers were idle in St Petersburg. The central European situation was not worth mentioning today, though an editorial in *The Times* about Poincare's visit to Russia said it 'should operate as a salutary warning to the 'war parties' in all the great countries against the danger of playing with fire.'

The Caillaux trial continued in Paris with dramatic interventions in all directions, straying into politics and allegations of secret documents found on the body of the late editor. France was transfixed (and to judge by the length of the reports in *The Times* and the other papers so was Britain).

Remarkably, Sydney Smith of Northamptonshire took four wickets in four balls against Warwickshire, only a few days after Alonzo Drake had done it. He and George Thompson bowled unchanged as Warwickshire made 103 and, following on, 76-2, but, as this was the last day, a draw was inevitable.

Colin Blythe reached 100 wickets for the season as Kent beat Gloucestershire. Yorkshire, surviving after being out for 75 on the first day, beat Nottinghamshire comfortably enough: Alonzo Drake should have had a hat trick but the third man was dropped at short leg. Rain ensured that Hampshire and Sussex drew at Southampton.

Captain K.R.McCloughlin made 112 for MCC against the Royal Engineers. He had played a few first-class matches, the first in Bombay in 1909. He died in France in November 1915.

Middlesex, with eight wins and no defeats in twelve matches, were still top of the table from Surrey, Kent and Hampshire.

The *Daily Express* sports page was decorated with a picture of 'sea nymphs at Brighton'. It remarked on S.G.Smith's four in four coming just a few days after Alonzo Drake's feat. The paper included results from the South London Cricket League (and probably a note of gloating in the report that the *Daily Herald's* team had been bowled out for 37 by Hardinge).

Now, on 24 July the Bayreuth Festival opened with *Der Fliegende Hollander* and *Parsifal*. Mme Gueydon, Caillaux's first wife, gave evidence on a day of 'dramatic incidents'. The drama was playing out to everyone's satisfaction, with gasps of amazement all round.

Austria-Hungary had delivered a formal note to Serbia. It gave Serbia 48 hours to comply with a list of demands with which it was practically certain Serbia would not comply.

The leaders of the St Petersburg strike had been arrested.

The Times continued to lead with the Buckingham Palace conference which now seemed likely to end in failure,

Several county games began on 23 July. Middlesex ran into trouble at Maidstone. They bowled Kent out for 265, but then slumped to 70-8, with seven wickets for Colin Blythe. At Southend Johnny Douglas put Sussex in to bat (most unusual in 1914) and bowled them out for 102, Bert Tremlin six for 52. Against Surrey at Portsmouth, the amateur Johnston and the professional Remnant put on 110, but they were all out for 202.

The Times gave the full scores for the 'Cock House' match at Harrow.

For the *Daily Express* the main story was the failure of the conference (hard pushed by Mme Caillaux). Page 2 was devoted to where to go on your summer holidays, complete with railway advertisements with timetables. The Brighton Railway and the South Eastern and Chatham offered trains to the continent and the Great Eastern offered trips to North Germany via Harwich and the Hook of Holland. The paper also ran a composite picture of five society ladies who had passed through the divorce courts the day before.

On 25 July it was reported that the Buckingham Palace conference had broken down and that was the main concern of *The Times*. The failure of the conference was attributed by the *Daily Express* to the 'radicals' and the 'hysterical spite' of the radical press. Suddenly, though, events in the Balkans were seen to be threatening.

> Austria-Hungary leaves a small and excitable Balkan kingdom to decide at a few hours' notice whether there is, or is not, to be a third Balkan War, and a Balkan war, this time, in which one of the great powers will be involved as a principal from the first,

said *The Times*. 'New European peril,' said the *Daily Express*. The Russians were leaning increasingly to support Serbia and *The Times* believed that Germany wanted to localise any conflict to the Balkans.

Middlesex had lost in two days and by an innings at Maidstone, Frank Woolley taking most of the second-innings wickets. Bowled out for 88 and 132, Middlesex did not look like potential champions, and the vagaries of the system now meant that Surrey were top. Derbyshire started badly at Northampton, losing six for 28 before struggling to 100. Sussex in their second innings at Southend managed 47 against Douglas and Tremlin, giving Essex their sixth win (in 1913 they had managed two). Remarkably enough, there were nine amateurs in the Essex team.

At Lord's the Royal Engineers played the Royal Artillery, (RE 68, RA 479 on day one). This match included the last known appearance of A.E.J. 'Boy' Collins, the man who at the age of 13 had made 628 not out in a junior house match at Clifton (still the highest known score in any form of cricket). Collins died at Ypres in November.

Lancashire and Yorkshire were meeting at Hull, in what was described as an 'extra match' (the word friendly perhaps not being entirely appropriate). Lancashire had made 259 and Yorkshire were 312-6 with Wilfred Rhodes 95 not out. The *Manchester Guardian* was not satisfied,

> The Lancashire and Yorkshire match at Hull might, up to a certain point yesterday afternoon, be fairly described as the drowsiest game the counties have played in years.

After the game it said that the first friendly, the previous year at Aigburth, was a 'magnificent game', but this year,

> The cricket was poor and lifeless, the spectators were few, the ground looked as if it wanted a thorough spring-cleaning, and when the rain mercifully put an end to it on Saturday probably no one, except the respective treasurers, was very sorry.

That day's cricket reports, however, were headed by 'First defeat for Middlesex'.

Somerset beat Worcestershire in two days at Stourbridge, with J.C.'Farmer'

White taking eleven wickets in the match (five for 25 and six for 66).

On 25 July WG played his last innings in any form of cricket. He scored 69 for Eltham against Grove Park. It was felt that had he been able to run he would have scored a century. He played in one further match on 8 August but was not required to bat in a drawn game between Eltham and Northbrook.

By now – for the first time – the leader column in *The Times* turned first to Europe rather than Ireland. The *Manchester Guardian* had started to worry earlier, talking on 25 July of a 'Grave European Crisis' and 'Threat of War'. 'Austria's note... has brought the continent to the verge of a great war'.

By this time things were stirring. The stock market was very depressed. The Serbian reply to the Austrian note had been delivered and was considered unsatisfactory. At this point the Austrian minister to Serbia left the country. The Serbian Army was mobilising. *The Times* took the view that the Serbian reply had been very moderate and conceded almost all that was asked,

> Surely the Emperor Francis Joseph, who has given the world so many proofs of his devotion to peace, is not going to jeopardize the safety of his empire and the tranquillity of Europe because Servia has not at once acceded to the whole of the very humiliating requirements of the note?

The paper talked of 'war fever' in Vienna and it now seemed hard to visualise how war could be avoided, with the question being how far it would spread; what would Russian commitments to Serbia and German commitments to Austria-Hungary mean in practice?

The trial of Mme Caillaux continued to give good value: the judge had apparently sent his seconds to the Assistant Judge because of 'certain remarks'. The lady herself had fainted when certain letters that M Caillaux had written to her were read out. The Admiralty cancelled leave for the Royal Navy. There were massive falls on the Berlin Bourse.

In Ireland an attempt at gun-running to the National Volunteers had resulted in a battle with the police and troops, with several dead. *The Times* said, 'there can be no doubt that the country is now confronted with one of the greatest crises in the history of the British race' – meaning, of course, Ireland. There was nothing to suggest any great popular reaction in England to either of these crises.

The Times noted that for the next ten days Lord's would be devoted to Public School cricket, leading up to the final match when a Schools XI would meet MCC. Surrey beat Hampshire by eight wickets and were now firmly top of the table. *The Times* also reported on the Bar v the Barristers' Clerks at the Oval. It indicates the extent to which such features as the cricket scores were about old school and varsity contacts and the gentlemanly classes talking to each other.

A meeting at Worcester showed the county in immediate need of £350 and apparently nowhere to go. A general meeting of members had been called. The *Daily Express* claimed that while county matches drew crowds of 500, 5,000 people were going to watch Worcester City FC in the Birmingham League.

On 28 July, with what at this distance seems considerable complacency, *The Times* suggested that 'the European situation is perceptibly less threatening than it was yesterday.' Sir Edward Grey, the Foreign Secretary, had said in Parliament that,

> The moment that this dispute ceases to be one between Austria-Hungary and Servia and involves another Great Power, it can but end in the greatest catastrophe that has ever befallen the continent of Europe at one blow.

The Times, even more complacently, felt that such a warning issued by a British foreign minister in the British parliament would bring Europe to its senses. It was, it reported, the cause of some relief in Paris. Later, though, it reported the air of crisis in Paris, with the foreign ministry staff all still at their posts and anti-war demonstrators (put down by *The Times* as 'syndicalists') in the streets.

The Times still believed, though, that Germany and France were 'sincerely working for peace' and that Austria-Hungary could be restrained. In many ways Ireland still looked a more precipitate danger, with shooting having started between troops and nationalists the day before.

It quoted the *New York Evening Post*, which appeared to look forward to a European war on the basis that it would leave the world open to American domination (which turned out to be the case, as faithfully recorded at the end of *1066 and All That*).

The *Daily Express* carried a substantial article by Lieutenant-Colonel Alsager Pollock,

> There are some people who fondly imagine that if a general war should break out in Europe this country might remain neutral. Such a delusion can seriously be indulged in by the insane.

Arthur William Alsager Pollock, aged 61, was to take his battalion to France and be gassed at Loos in 1915, though he subsequently returned to HQ. It seems slightly odd for a serving soldier to express such a forthright opinion. Still, however, the paper's main leader was about Ireland.

Still there were more things in France to get excited about. M Caillaux had somehow got hold of a copy of the will of M Calmette, the deceased editor. This may or may not have been relevant in scenes more and more reminiscent of *Alice in Wonderland* as M Bernstein, the playwright, also made a dramatic intervention.

On the Stock Exchange there was a slight rally late in the day but shares had been 'very depressed'.

The cricket page in *The Times* began with an article about the question of coaching at public schools (following the tetchy correspondence about Harrow). It followed that with Clifton v Tonbridge. Tonbridge were out for 55 after the first four batsmen got ducks. Clifton made 266 and Tonbridge were 73-4. G.W.E.Whitehead had a good day, taking three for 9, making 78 and then taking three more wickets. George Whitehead played a couple of games for Kent this year, but died near Menin in October 1918.

Then only did *The Times* turn to county cricket. For Essex C.A.G.'Jack' Russell, a steady professional batsman who was later to play a handful of Test matches and to average over 50 in them, and C.D.McIver, who had won Oxford blues in 1903 and 1904 and played 59 matches for Essex over 20 years, set a new county record with an opening stand of 212 against Leicestershire. Essex ended the day at 428 all out.

Surrey's push for the title continued as Sussex were out for 184 at the Oval, Surrey 114-2 at the close. There were wickets for G.J.W.Platt, a professional who played 33 times between 1906 and 1914, taking over 100 wickets, and later playing for Staffordshire.

By 29 July hopes of peace were dashed as Austria-Hungary formally declared war on Serbia. *The Times* was now arguing (with the benefit of a little hindsight) that Austria had played it that way all along and had never intended to be dissuaded from war. This was almost certainly correct, though Austria's war aims were very vague: Austria was insistent that it had no territorial demands (and indeed the last thing the rickety empire needed was more troublesome Slav subjects), but it certainly wanted to give Serbia a good thumping and hopefully to divide the country up. But *The Times* still argued that Russian movements were essentially defensive and that Germany 'had behaved very well' being 'dragged at the heels of the Austrian war chariot'. France was taking precautions. The *Manchester Guardian* was still suggesting that Austria and Russia could show sense even after Austria-Hungary's declaration of war. On 30 July it said,

> *The Times*, whose influence at great crises in our foreign affairs has almost always been for evil, yesterday took it for granted that if the war were not localised this country ought to take the side of Servia and Russia.

There were those who still believed that war could be prevented. The International Socialist Bureau would meet in Brussels. Jean Jaurès had issued a statement that held the Austro-Hungarian government responsible, agreeing that France was doing what she could to avoid war. In Britain precautionary measures were being taken but the government was not talking much about them. France and Italy were prepared to attend an ambassadorial meeting in London, but Germany had not given a positive response. *The Times'* Paris correspondent had reason to believe that Germany 'has given more proofs of her desire for peace than have yet become known to the French.'

Slightly overshadowed at last (though in France the papers gave it more space than the impending crisis) was the trial and Mme Caillaux's sensational acquittal on the grounds that M Calmette had insulted her husband's honour and that she had done what any good wife would do. The British press marvelled at the strange ways of foreigners.

Against Essex's 428, Leicestershire managed 92 against Douglas and Tremlin, but they were 276-2 at the second attempt with Sam Coe unbeaten on 135. At the Oval Sussex offered slightly stiffer resistance after starting their second innings 77 behind and losing 6-75, then recovering to 225 all out so at least setting a target. J.,H.Vincett, who had already taken five for 32, made 73. At Trent Bridge John Gunn made 142 not out against Kent to give Nottinghamshire a substantial lead.

The *Daily Express* reported that A.P.Freeman had taken five for 6 for Kent II against Staffordshire, bowled out for 85 for a substantial Kent win (Freeman had five for 57 in the first innings) The paper also listed the players going on tour with Blackheath Wanderers to South Devon.

By 30 July, hostilities had broken out between Austria and Serbia.

The Times reported a huge demand for insurance against war risks, even though rates had tripled or even quadrupled. Business was about to be suspended on the German stock exchange. In a small piece the paper announced that the fortresses at Liege and Namur were now on a war footing. President Poincare had returned from his visit to St Petersburg. The *France* had passed a German torpedo boat near Kiel and had ritually exchanged salutes. At the Gare du Nord the President was met by a large crowd cheering and singing the Marseillaise. Despite occasional cries of 'Vive la guerre!' *The Times* stressed that the demonstration was patriotic rather than warlike. Russia was still biding her time. But on all sides armies were lumbering into action, and there was a feeling that the process might have become automatic and unstoppable. Mr Asquith had said that the situation was one of 'extreme gravity'.

It was reported from Berlin that the German attitude was that the Austro-Serbian situation was past saving, that relations between Austria and Russia were their own business, but Russian mobilisation posed a threat. There was no talk of Western Europe. Albanians in Kosovo were threatening to join in against Serbia.

The Stock Exchange had gone to pieces at this stage with as many as seven members hammered, though things calmed down as the day went on.

The Times said, 'Europe is on the verge of a war more general and more terrible than the 'Great War' of one hundred years ago.' If France or the Belgian frontier was menaced 'we shall know how to act'.

Surrey indeed beat Sussex, but what had looked like a formality ended as a win by one wicket as they went from 133-5 to 145-9 in pursuit of 149. K.H.C.Woodroffe took six for 43, almost snatching victory. This was Kenneth Woodroffe's best performance of a short career. He had just come down from his second year at Cambridge, winning blues in both years, and had played for Hampshire against the South Africans in 1912 while still at school, taking five for 33. This was his first game for Sussex, his county of birth. He died near Neuve Chapelle in May 1915.

Essex beat Leicestershire, despite the county making 521 in the second innings (Sam Coe out for 152). Essex got the 186 they needed with the help of 65 from Captain W.M.Turner. Nottinghamshire, needing only 101 to beat Kent, were bowled out for 53 by Blythe (five for 32) and Woolley (five for 20).

Reginald Ashfield made 130 for Marlborough against Rugby at Lord's. He was still at school and after the war appeared once for Cambridge University in a non-first-class match.

The *Daily Express* said that there were nearly 10,000 at Blackheath to see Kent play Surrey where Wally Hardinge made 86. Without making a great impact on the season, he was to be one of *Wisden's* Five for 1915.

Even the *Express* still gives a full score for Marlborough v Rugby. In a minor counties match at the Oval, Staffordshire made 371 against Surrey II with hundreds from B.Meakin and L.F.Taylor. Bernard Meakin had played once for Gloucestershire (when at school at Clifton) and a couple of times for Cambridge University (without getting a blue), but was a Staffordshire stalwart until 1922. Leonard Taylor played only for Staffordshire (though he was qualifying for Warwickshire) and was to die in France in March 1917. Staffordshire went on to win by an innings in a game in which Barnes only took four wickets.

A report in the *Daily Express* discussed the marriage of John Freeman-Mitford (an uncle of the Mitford sisters) to the former Fraulein von Friedlander-Fuld who was apparently living apart from him. The *Sporting Times* had apparently suggested that this was after he had committed 'unnatural offences' against her. The divorce courts (while effectively available only to the wealthy) were an endless source of salacious fun. At the same time the paper was shocked by the acquittal of Mme Caillaux and greatly impressed by Rolf the wonder dog of Mannheim.

By 31 July, with serious trouble looming, even the Unionist party and the Ulstermen (given their presented position as patriots) had to come onside. Germany had not mobilised – yet – but was imminently expected to do so. Austria was advancing into Serbia and Belgrade was being shelled [note that this involved an attack on the civilian population – Germany was not the first]. Sir Edward Grey had made a new offer of mediation, but it did not seem to be attracting any takers. In Britain the Territorial Special Reserve was being called to the colours.

In the City, two more firms were hammered: there were heavy falls on the New York exchange.

Surrey were playing at Kent at Blackheath knowing that a Kent victory would push them down to third place. Kent, batting down the order, made 349 but Hayward and Hobbs had taken Surrey briskly to 57-0 by the close. At Brighton, Northamptonshire scored 435-3 against Sussex, with S.G.Smith unbeaten on 159. Lancashire played Warwickshire at Lune Road, Lancaster (the first and only first-class match on the ground). Warwickshire made 335-9 with centuries from W.G.Quaife and C.S.Baker. William Quaife was already 42 and had been a *Wisden* cricketer of the year in 1902, but would play for the county until 1928. Charles Baker left Warwickshire after 1920, playing for Cornwall and pursuing a career as a cartoonist.

Somerset and Derbyshire at Taunton played like a one-day match – Derbyshire 63 and 93-5, Somerset 100. E.Robson took seven for 32 in Derbyshire's first innings and had taken two in the second. Robson, a right-arm-fast-medium bowler and a Yorkshireman, was 44 years old and was to carry on after the war.

Rugby beat Marlborough at Lord's, Marlborough being out for 82 in their second innings.

On Friday 31 July the *Aberdeen Journal* reported that during a cricket match at Cork, the soldiers taking part were called off and the match abandoned.

The bank holiday weekend was about to begin.

Chapter 7

August 1914

Saturday 1 August was the first day of the bank holiday weekend. Most of the traditional 'holiday' matches then started on the Monday.

Cole & Postgate[27] suggest the air of unreality about the outbreak of war was added to by the fact that the vital events took place over a bank holiday weekend: the *Daily Mail* might be shouting for war, but then it did, and the man in the street did not know the ramifications of the *Entente Cordiale* and the rather vague promises that had been made about Belgian neutrality.

Russia was now mobilising completely and Germany was under martial law (except for Bavaria, still regarded as a quasi-independent kingdom). Holland and Belgium were mobilising, and France heading that way. *The Times* thought there was still some faint hope that disaster would be averted.

At this point, with France in something of a dither, Jean Jaurés, probably France's or even Europe's best-known and most respected politician of the left, was murdered as he sat at a café in Montmartre. It all added to the feeling that things were out of control.

There seemed to be movement on all the potential war fronts: every border reported troop movements.

In America, the sailing of German transatlantic liners was suspended, effectively impounding the *Vaterland* and the *Amerika*, both of which would end up with new names in American hands.

The Foreign Office suggested that continental travel for Britons might be inconvenienced, though they anticipated no danger. The King had sent messages to the Tsar and the Kaiser (all being family business).

In the city all was chaos – the bank rate doubled from 4 to 8% and stock exchange business was paralysed.

The Times was preparing a special Sunday edition in case of significant news. The *Daily Express* came over all high-minded,

> In view of the gravity of the situation the *Express* has decided not to publish any news affecting British naval and military movements and preparations which might in the slightest degree cause inconvenience to the authorities. Only purely official information issued by the Admiralty and the War Office will find room in these columns while the

---

27   *The Common People 1746-1938*, Methuen, 1938, (p 491)

crisis lasts. We deem this declaration to be due to our readers in view of the ill-advised reports which have in the last few days appeared in several newspapers. We prefer to withhold news which might give information to a possible enemy.

The anti-war movement, such as it was, mainly Quakers and Socialists, would fade away or be overwhelmed, with the more significant politicians deeming it right or expedient to follow the flag, or at least feeling that that once the boys were over there they had to be supported.

The *Dartford Chronicle* reported on a notice on a park gate saying that a meeting would be held on Monday evening (August 3) asking the public to support a resolution calling on the government to adopt an attitude of neutrality. After waiting a considerable time for an audience which did not assemble, the speakers decided to abandon the meeting. It was, of course, too late by then.

Ben Steward, who was working in an office at Tilbury Docks, said,

It seemed an ordinary August bank holiday in 1914.

It was sunny and warm. I spent it at Mundesley bathing and playing cricket on the beach with school friends.

The sun shone on young men and their sweethearts everywhere. Millions of them. They had hardly a care in the world. Nor had I. Later that day, August 3rd, my train to London was crowded and slow and often halted, to let some troop trains go through, we were told. At half past one in the morning of Tuesday, August 4th, we arrived hours late at Liverpool Street station. Just another end to another holiday, it seemed, with trains running late. Nobody worried very much.[28]

At Lord's the public schools played on. Cheltenham scored 331 against Haileybury, G.S.Lightfoot 120. Gordon Lightfoot played just this one year for Cheltenham, during which he turned 17: nothing more seems to be known about him. At the Oval Surrey powered on to 488-7, with hundreds for Hayward, Hobbs and Knight. At Taunton Robson took another seven wickets to bowl Derbyshire out, giving him 14 for the match. Essex took a substantial lead against Hampshire and by the close were 363 ahead with four wickets left.

Lionel Tennyson recalled that he was staying in his flat at Princes Hotel in Piccadilly, preparatory to taking part in the August Bank Holiday match against Essex at Leyton the next day, when at two in the morning the night porter brought him a message to say that war had been declared and that he must return to duty immediately. The story is slightly spoiled by the fact that the Essex game from which Tennyson had stepped down to join his regiment actually started on 31 July[29].

Yorkshire wrapped up Gloucestershire by an innings and 118 at Harrogate. For Warwickshire, Jeeves and Foster bowled Lancashire out for 128.

---

28   B.A.Steward, *One Journey*, self-published, 1981.
29   Lionel, Lord Tennyson, *From Verse To Worse*, Cassell, 1933

The *Daily Express* provided a lot of information. This Saturday, not only were the usual cricket scores there, but for the bank holiday weekend there was a long list of 'where to go for the best cricket matches' including a very long list of club fixtures, the South London League, the Harrow and Wealdstone League, and the Battersea Churches Association games on Wandsworth Common.

The racing at Goodwood was 'largely spoiled by the absence of a large number of officers of both Services through anticipation of recall to their ships or regiments'. The reports in the newspapers concentrated on describing the ladies' dresses.

On Sunday 2 August, *The Times* indeed printed a special edition of eight pages. The news was that Germany had declared war on Russia and German troops had invaded Luxembourg and – in the latest reports – France. The bank rate was raised to 10%. There were treaty obligations to do with the neutrality of Luxembourg, though nobody had responded as yet (and never would – this seemed to be the last time anyone mentioned Luxembourg). British involvement was not inevitable, but it was getting very close.

The 3rd was August Bank Holiday Monday. The leading news was – at last – the war. The actual war news was much the same as yesterday's – Germany had declared war on Russia and had invaded Luxembourg and France. Word from Russia was that they were awaiting Britain's decision.

Sir Ernest Shackleton's *Endurance* had set out on the first leg of the Imperial Trans-Antarctic Expedition – but would not actually leave Britain for several days (Winston Churchill had been consulted and had said 'go'). The report said that arrangements had been made for the King to meet them at Cowes – but that might now be Buckingham Palace as the regatta had been cancelled.

The Times said, 'War has come upon Europe so swiftly that few understand how or why': a statement that could still be made about that time today. The assassination in Sarajevo had provided the 'merest pretext' for attempting to obtain Austro-German control of the Balkans, Asia Minor and the sea routes to Egypt and Italy. But there were still those who wrote to the paper arguing that Britain could stay out of what was still largely a Balkan conflict.

The *Daily Express* was in no doubt. Blazed across the top of the front page was, 'Is Britain to stand dishonoured before the world?' The paper was now all for war in support of France. There was no mention of Belgium. There was, however, still room to report that the restaurants of London were being swept clean of staff as the waiters were called up by their lands – 140 (mainly French and 80 of them cooks) from the Savoy alone. Service, it said, was slow: the quality of cooking was not mentioned.

The cabinet had met twice; the second time after news came of the German moves against Luxembourg and France, and had apparently come to a decision which would be announced "today".

Railway companies were cancelling their excursion trains, and the boat train had left Victoria full of émigrés returning to the Continent and no English holiday-makers. The Cowes Regatta had been cancelled, but other sport was at this time untouched and the bank-holiday cricket programme would continue. The Canterbury Week would go on, but the traditional accompanying theatrical performance by the Old Stagers was in doubt as several of the actors were soldiers who might now have other duties.

Robert Graves wrote in *Goodbye To All That* (published in 1929), 'the papers predicted a very short war – over by Christmas at the outside', but any source for that famous phrase is hard to pin down.

Kent and Surrey had drawn at Blackheath on the Saturday when rain had ended play at about five o'clock with Kent 100 ahead with three wickets left. Hampshire had held out for a draw against Essex with B.G.von B. Melle taking five for 73 and then making 42* as part of a match-saving partnership with Alec Bowell. Basil George von Brandis Melle was a South African in his second year at Oxford and who was to play the odd game for the county until 1921. Sussex, one wicket left and 77 runs away from an innings defeat, were saved by the rain against Northamptonshire. Warwickshire beat Lancashire and Somerset beat Derbyshire.

Surrey, Middlesex and Kent filled the first three places in the Championship with Hampshire still clinging to fourth place.

It must have been very strange watching – or indeed playing – cricket on that Bank Holiday Monday. As well as the scorecard sellers there would have been the newspaper vendors. Everyone knew that Parliament was going to take a crucial decision that day, and while war was still not inevitable it was exceedingly probable. At this time, remarkably, there had still been no mention of Belgium.

You might have gone to Derby or Bristol, Southampton or Canterbury, Old Trafford or Northampton, the Oval or Edgbaston: all sixteen counties were in action simultaneously. It might have been the treat you were looking forward to for weeks. Or you could be going out to open the batting wondering whether war would have been declared by the time you were out. Everyone must have known that it was overwhelmingly probable that Europe was headed down the slippery slope and pulling Britain along as well.

A couple of extra days had been added to the bank holiday (for the benefit of the banks, not the workers). Britain was mobilising.

On 4 August, *The Times* was a slim ten pages (but because of the bank holiday rather than the war). It reported the movement of French troops to the frontier and skirmishes to the East. But at 7.00 pm the previous evening Germany had delivered an ultimatum to Belgium offering to respect Belgian neutrality if Belgium allowed the passage of German troops through the country. Belgium was understood to have refused the offer. *The Times* pointed out that by a treaty of 1839 we were obliged to act if Belgian neutrality was violated.

The Times did have room for a comment on 'the servant problem' but it was basically a plug for *The Times'* own advertising service.

At Canterbury the Old Stagers, as feared, had cancelled. About 7,000 people turned up for the start of the Canterbury Week, though 'the club tents were sparsely populated.' Sussex were 327-4 after the first day, Joe Vine, whose long Sussex career would continue until 1922, making 140.

Over 14,000 people were there at the Oval to see Hobbs make 226 (in 260 minutes) as Surrey reached 472-5 against Nottinghamshire. At Old Trafford play did not start until 3.00 pm by which time the Lancashire captain, A.H.Hornby, had to leave 'in answer to a call from the War Office' and Reggie Spooner took over the captaincy. Rhodes, Hirst and Drake bowled Lancashire out for 162.

The Times gave a full score for the match between Lord's Schools and The Rest, but restricted the county championship games to summarised scores. At Derby Mr J.Chapman, fielding for Derbyshire, was also called away by the War Office 'in connection with the purchase of Army horses' and H.Wild was allowed to take his place. John Chapman had been the club captain from 1910 to 1912 and would be again after the War. The current captain, R.R.C.Baggallay, was a gentleman but a player of no great distinction – his career average was 11.86. He won both the MC and DSO.

On 5 August, the news was that war had been declared. Germany had not responded to the note about Belgian neutrality and so the formal declaration of war was as from 11 pm on 4 August. *The Times* immediately insisted that Germany had been planning this for years (striking quite a different note from a few days before).

Across the top of the *Daily Express* it said, 'England expects that every man will do his duty.' War had been declared. 'Stopping the world's bully', said the *Express.*

So what did this mean to people on the street or at the cricket? There had been wars since the final defeat of Napoleon in 1815, but they had either been far distant or Britain had not been involved. British troops had not fought in Europe since 1815. The colonial or the Crimean, even the Boer War, had not greatly disturbed the tenor of life at home. So if you were a professional cricketer on 5 August you would have turned up for work as you might at the foundry or the office. It was not for you to suggest that the office might be closed.

The early impact was felt as at least five county captains, Sir Archibald White (Yorkshire), A.H.Hornby (Lancashire), Pelham Warner (Middlesex), Arthur Carr (Nottinghamshire) and R.R.C.Baggallay (Derbyshire) left the scene to join their regiments. None of them, apart from Warner who made one appearance against Surrey later in the month, played after 5 August. They were to be followed by a sixth: H.P.Chaplin was called away during Sussex's match against Middlesex which started on 6 August.

In *Memoirs of a Fox-hunting Man*, Siegfried Sassoon as George Sherston says,

Many of us believed that the Russians would occupy Berlin (and perhaps catch the Kaiser) before Christmas. The newspapers informed us that German soldiers crucified Belgian babies. Stories of that kind were taken for granted: to have disbelieved them would have been unpatriotic.[30]

Bertrand Russell was surprised,

During the hot days at the end of July, I was at Cambridge, discussing the situation with all and sundry. I found it impossible to believe that Europe would be so mad as to plunge into war, but I was persuaded that, if there was a war, England would be involved. I felt strongly that England ought to remain neutral, and I collected the signatures of a large number of Professors and Fellows to a statement which appeared in the *Manchester Guardian* to that effect. The day war was declared, almost all of them changed their minds.[31]

Neville Cardus said in his autobiography that when war broke out he immediately offered himself to the army but to neither his surprise nor dismay he was turned down because of short-sightedness. He was coaching at Shrewsbury School that summer and at this point became the Headmaster's secretary (his predecessor having enlisted).

For the moment all regular reservists were required to proceed immediately to the place of joining on their identity certificates and those on leave were recalled. The two super-Dreadnoughts being built for Turkey were commandeered for the Royal Navy instead.

The Times was heavily promoting the cause of Lord Kitchener as Minister for War.

The Kent County Cricket Club put out a statement. It read,

The committee of the Kent CCC trust that the public will not suppose that in deciding as far as lies in their power to adhere to the programme of matches they are indifferent to the grave crisis which affects the country. Their decision is due to their solicitude for the club's employees, whose earnings would be materially affected if county matches were not played.

Dover Week would be played, but luncheon would not be provided for the public (though presumably it would for the members).

But reports here were for the cricket played on the last day of peace. At Canterbury, during the afternoon, the Band of the 6th Dragoon Guards played the *Marseillaise* and the Russian National Anthem. Sussex went on to 384 and Kent were all out for 291.

The Oval was to be taken over immediately for military purposes, so there would presumably be no more cricket there once the ongoing match was over. Surrey reached 542 and Nottinghamshire were 230-5. Barrackers

---

30   Siegfried Sassoon, Memoirs of a Fox-Hunting Man, Faber & Faber, 1942, p201.
31   Bertrand Russell, Autobiography, George Allan & Unwim 1968 volume 2 p.15

were ejected from the ground during a slow partnership between George Gunn and Joe Hardstaff. For this and all other matches only summarised scores were provided by *The Times*. Gloucestershire v Somerset at Bristol hurtled to a conclusion: Somerset 82 and 105, Gloucestershire 111 and 77-9. In this match (Gloucestershire's only victory in 1914) the Somerset innings was opened by the twin brothers A.D.E.(Dudley) and A.E.S (Sydney) Rippon, typical Somerset amateurs who attended King's College, Taunton and not gone to university. Neither was a cricketer of great distinction. Sydney's son Geoffrey became a Tory MP.

At Old Trafford Drake and Rhodes bowled Lancashire out for 83 and Yorkshire, needing 51 to win, were 5-0.

Essex bowled Derbyshire out for 31 and 94 to win by an innings and 131: in the day Douglas took nine for 62, Tremlin ten for 52 including a first-innings hat trick.

On 6 August *The Times* reported that the German invasion of Belgium had been repulsed at all points. The official announcement said, 'We are completely victorious'. This was, as it happens, completely untrue. It was also reported that five German spies dressed as priests had been arrested at the Gare du Nord in Brussels. That might not have been true either.

Today it was reported that Kitchener had indeed been appointed as Secretary of State for War. His post of Agent and Consul-General in Egypt would be kept open in case he was able to return to it shortly.

Sussex beat Kent at Canterbury by 34 runs, G.R.Cox taking six for 45. 'Old' George Cox played for Sussex from 1895 to 1928, and his son, 'Young George', from 1931 to 1960.

All other games were drawn as rain closed in, except that Northamptonshire beat Leicestershire by four runs, Leicestershire collapsing to 79 all out. In a low-scoring game the last two Northamptonshire wickets had put on 62. Surrey and Nottinghamshire managed only three-quarters of an hour and as the first innings of each side had not been completed the game did not count for championship points.

The *Manchester Guardian* said on 6 August, 'the war is already having its effect on cricket' with various amateurs off to join their regiments and Kent II left to bat one short against Staffordshire as Lowe had left to join the colours as a reservist.

The funeral of Albert Trott, 'the famous Middlesex and Australian cricketer,' was reported. Trott's suicide was a great shock: he had, of course, played Test cricket for both Australia and England and had then had a long and illustrious career with Middlesex.

On 7 August Kitchener's call for 100,000 men topped the front page of the *Daily Express*. At the bottom of the page a little box urges every able-bodied man under 35 to step forward (oddly since Kitchener's limit at this point was 30).

The Times reports a 'rush to serve' at the recruiting office at Great Scotland

Yard. There were complaints from East Anglia - raised in the House of Commons - that horses needed for the harvest were being requisitioned, though they were supposed to be exempt until the harvest was over. It was admitted that two of the forts defending Liege had fallen and that the Belgians were preparing to defend the town by street fighting.

Race meetings at Folkestone, Lewes and Redcar had been cancelled because of the demand made on the railways - which had immediately been brought under state control - for national purposes.

Mr F.E.Lacey, Secretary of MCC, said,

> The secretary of MCC feels that no good purpose can be served at the present moment by cancelling matches unless the services of those engaged in cricket who have no military training can in any way be utilized in their country's service. If it can be shown in what way their services can be used the MCC would close their ground. Many out matches have already been abandoned. Cricketers of England would be sure to respond to any definite call,

The abandonment of MCC's out matches was probably for logistical reasons. Picking up scratch teams of gentlemen would have been impossibly difficult as they returned to the colours. MCC played no games after 20 August and 22 were cancelled.

A further indication was the cancellation of I Zingari's seven remaining fixtures of which three were against military sides.

Once again *The Times* gave summarised scores and sometimes a very brief account of highlights on a day when most matches were spoiled by rain. There was not time for much but W.Brown took seven for 51 for Leicestershire against Derbyshire at Leicester. William Brown was a left-arm slow medium bowler who played 46 games for Leicestershire between 1910 and 1919, and this was his best match. B.G.von B. Melle had taken the field for Hampshire against Nottinghamshire, but received orders to return to his regiment and was replaced.

The Prince of Wales, it was reported, would be given a commission in the Grenadier Guards, join them forthwith, and go on active service.

On 8 August, Liege was reported to be holding on. It was also said that the Germans had lost 25,000 men in the assault. As *The Times* said,

> the estimate of the German losses is greatly exaggerated, or it gives the measure of wholesale slaughter to be expected in this war. We greatly prefer the former explanation.

In fact both legs of the statement were correct. *The Daily Express* was in no doubt,' 'The Mad Dog held up at Liege', it claimed. MCC were playing London Clubs at Lord's - MCC were whipped out the next day for 62 by Richard Bell who hadn't played a first-class match for six years and then only a handful, and W.Ransom, otherwise unknown.

Banks were reopening today and the new £1 note appeared for the first time, replacing the gold sovereign. There was agreement across the country with the trade unions – strikes were ended in the London building trades and various active demands were withdrawn across the country.

The Admiralty and the War Office had set up an official news bureau (not to disseminate news so much as to control it). The German consul in Sunderland had been arrested and charged with something unspecified.

More race meetings had been abandoned and a general suspension was expected (as had already happened in France).

It was reported that the pavilion at Trent Bridge had been commandeered by the War Office for the wounded: in practice this did not happen right away and Nottinghamshire were able to complete their fixtures.

Mr F.H.Bacon, the Hampshire secretary, was suggesting the formation of a squad of professional cricketers for home defence, and said that all the Hampshire professionals had agreed that they would join such a squad.

The county scores were provided in brief. Kent (301) beat Northamptonshire (70 and 179) by an innings, Blythe and Woolley taking the wickets. Yorkshire beat Warwickshire. Essex had replied to Lancashire's 179 with 386-8, with centuries for Douglas and J.R.Freeman, brother of the ultimately more famous 'Tich'. John Freeman played for Essex from 1905 to 1928. A.P. was shortly to make his championship debut, though a Kent team with Blythe and Woolley seemed in little need of another spinner.

Middlesex replied to Sussex's 411 (Relf had made 150) with 293-8. H.P.Chaplin, the Sussex captain, was summoned by the War Office during the game and was replaced by H.E.Roberts as a full substitute (though in fact he neither batted nor bowled). Chaplin was effectively in his last years of first-class cricket, but his last recorded appearance on CricketArchive was for his own XI against Sussex in a one-day game in 1943 when he was 60 years old. In that game he had the nous to pick the young Alec Bedser who took eight for 43.

Surrey had gained a substantial lead against Worcestershire, though a second-innings collapse for 147 against F.A.Pearson (six for 55) left Worcestershire with 251 to win. Fred Pearson played for Worcestershire from 1900 to 1926, yet another long-life professional: he had also played three games for Auckland in 1910/11 taking 21 wickets. Hampshire were being routed by Nottinghamshire, replying to 341 with 103 and 111-5. Hampshire's team was by now shorn of all its military men, and somewhat weakened. They were already without Johnston, Greig and Tennyson while Melle was summoned from the game. Hampshire, incidentally, had no spare men to hand and had to send for Stone and A.C.P.Arnold.

Leicestershire, chasing 205 against Derbyshire, were 83-6.

10 August came, and Liege was still said to be holding out gallantly, and indeed *The Times* suggested that the Germans had been 'handsomely beaten.' The *Daily Express* was even more sure – 'Germans routed in Alsace', it said.

Twice, it was claimed, the Germans had asked for an armistice and that their losses were very heavy. This, despite the fact that it was admitted that Liege was now completely surrounded.

Heavy rain had prevented or severely restricted play in all Saturday's matches, and none of them produced results. *The Times* showed the top six in the Championship, with Surrey leading, Middlesex second and Kent third. Seven matches were due to start today. Middlesex had decided at one point to call off the match with Yorkshire at Bramall Lane, but then managed to scrape a team together.

The Somerset v Northamptonshire game at Taunton which should have started on 10 August was called off 'because of the war' but details are vague and *The Times* never mentions it. It is likely to have been due to amateurs disappearing for military duty, as Somerset were heavily dependent on their gentlemen members.

In the *Yorkshire Post* Old Ebor felt things should carry on,

> One of the normal features of British life is, of course, the support of such pastimes as cricket and football, and it does seem a question whether it is wise to remove these from a sphere of activities just at a time when many thousands of the public will have too many hours for idleness and fretting on their hands.

All the war news on 11 August appeared to be good. 500,000 to 600,000 men had been mobilised for the Army with recruits 'pouring in faster than they can be examined.' The Russians were said to be advancing. The French were moving into Alsace. Liege was untaken and could probably hold out for some time.

There was a call for young men to take temporary commissions, asking that 'Cadets or ex-cadets of a University Training Corps or members of a University should apply to their commanding officer. Other young men of good general education should apply to the officer commanding the nearest depot.' They would serve for the duration of the war.

Surrey were playing Kent at Lord's (The Oval having been requisitioned) and it was Jack Hobbs' benefit match. Hobbs later wrote that all that time he had been looking forward to his benefit match which would be against Kent. He felt that he had every reason to anticipate a good match. Surrey were prospective champions and centuries were coming freely. He recalled how when Surrey played Nottinghamshire at the Oval on the Bank Holiday Monday the papers were full of war talk but that a crowd of 17,000 followed the game with the keenest interest. He said, ' I made 226 with never the thought of war. Those were the days when nobody had any idea of what it was all to mean.' On the next day the Secretary told him that the Oval had been commandeered. Hobbs continued,

> The Committee were very sympathetic, and told me that the Kent and Yorkshire matches would be played at Lord's in the following week. They gave me the option of postponing my benefit until after the War,

or of taking it at Lord's.[32]

The attendance was estimated at 7,000 and a collection produced £24/14/6. The result was something of a disaster for Hobbs. Although Surrey guaranteed £500, the total receipts from his benefit came to £657, below the average level, let alone what might have been expected. The Surrey committee agreed that he would be granted another chance the following year or, failing that, once the war had ended.[33]

In the match, Kent had lost 4 for 11 but rallied somewhat to 140. Surrey were 147-3, though Hobbs was out for 16.

On 12 August the response to Lord Kitchener's appeal was said to be satisfactory, with an average of 3,000 a day signing up: but *The Times* felt the need to encourage the wealthy to relinquish some of their servants.

The *Daily Express* proclaimed the 'Eve of the Great Battle'.

Surrey won in two days, Hitch and Fender bowling Kent out for 140 and 140, though Blythe took nine for 97. Surrey made 234 (Hayward 91) and 47-2 to win by eight wickets. 7,046 paid for admission. Middlesex were struggling against Yorkshire, having made 175 and 219-6 against 345 (David Denton 129). Denton was 40 years old but would play on for a couple of seasons after the war.

Frank Chester made 178* for Worcestershire against Essex, his highest first-class score. Losing an arm at Salonika during the war, he became an umpire and stayed at it until 1955. Harry Dean took 13 wickets in the match as Lancashire beat Hampshire by an innings, and Nottinghamshire beat Gloucestershire by an innings as well.

The Portsmouth Cricket Week had been called off as the military had taken over the ground, with the two matches arranged transferred to Southampton and Bournemouth.

There was news of a couple of German bakers' shops in the East End being wrecked (though *The Times* was quick to assure its readers that the perpetrators could not have been Englishmen.

Many places were keen to emphasise that for seaside holidays it was business as usual and that the trains were not much affected – the Isle of Wight, Scarborough, Torquay and Felixstowe were all keen to say that they were open for holiday business.

The Times remarked that much of what the new official Press Bureau gave out as news had already been reported. At this period, said *The Times*, 'no news of any importance can be expected.' The papers would not, for instance, give information about British troop movements. Liege was reported still to be holding out.

On 13 August *The Times* was again encouraging holiday makers: railway companies which had suspended cheap fares were thinking of

32   Jack Hobbs, *My Cricket Memories*, London, 1924
33   Leo McKinstry, Jack Hobbs, *England's Greatest Cricketer*, Yellow Jersey, 2012

reintroducing them. *The Daily Express* was full of advertisements from railway companies and seaside towns imploring people to go on holiday, but cricket was still only a single column.

There was an advertisement for the 'standard history' of the Great War, to begin in weekly sixpenny parts next Monday. It would be edited by H.W.Wilson, the author of *With the Flag to Pretoria*. Wilson was the chief leader writer of the *Daily Mail* and co-author with William le Queux of a novel called *The Invasion of 1910* (published in 1906).

The Times reported that the Germans had marched on Liege wearing uniforms stolen from the bodies of dead Belgian soldiers.

Yorkshire (who had started the season badly) attained their eighth consecutive victory, beating Middlesex by two wickets. Only an innings of 121 by Hendren had set a target at all, and it was only 89, but they just made it. Ashley-Cooper's *History of Middlesex* complained that' there can be little doubt that, but for some of its members having answered the call to arms upon the outbreak of war, Middlesex would have been champion county' Before the game the Middlesex committee had wired Yorkshire to say that 'so many of their essential players being otherwise engaged on account of the war' they would be unable to fulfil the engagement, but changed their mind the same day.[34]

The players missing would appear to have been W.P.Robertson, E.S.Littlejohn, F.T.Mann and N.E.Haig (all amateurs). Littlejohn (a doctor) only played in six matches and did not reappear after the war, but the others were regulars and serious losses to the team. Apart from Harry Lee, the replacements were all amateurs – G.L.Hebden, C.A.Saville and C.A.Saville. Clifford Saville's three games in August were his only first-class appearances; he was killed on the Western Front in 1917.

Sussex beat Leicestershire by 221 runs and Worcestershire drew with Essex. Yorkshire had moved up to fourth, but Surrey were now looking difficult to beat.

It was reported on 14 August that the Mayor of Deal had been arrested on Dover cliffs on suspicion of being a spy, but was identified by a local tradesman. The London, Brighton and South Coast Railway had resumed the sale of cheap tickets. The *Daily Express* headline was 'Do not shout until you are out of the wood'. This appears to be a suggestion that the Germans are being beaten in Belgium. The paper also suggested that valuable racehorses stabled at Newmarket and owned by foreigners could be liable to seizure (what use highly strung thoroughbreds would have been is another matter).

Following numerous reports of Belgian victories, it was admitted that the Germans were a lot closer to Brussels.

At Lord's, on 13 August, Surrey scored 434-3 against Yorkshire, Hayward and Hobbs opening with 290 (Hayward 116, Hobbs 202). 30 wickets fell in

---

34   F.S.Ashley-Cooper, *Middlesex County Cricket Club 1906-1920*,

the day at Edgbaston, Warwickshire 111 and 78, Kent 111. A.P.Freeman in only the second championship match of his astonishing career took seven for 25 (five bowled, none stumped!) in the first Warwickshire innings. The report in the (Birmingham-based) *Evening Despatch* said that Freeman mainly achieved his result by flight 'though strangely enough turning the ball where Blythe and Woolley could not.' Fielder took seven for 34 in the Warwickshire second innings.

Lancashire were all out for 342 against Middlesex (Sharp 120). Hampshire, sliding away after good early-season form, were all out for 91 at Chesterfield.

The *Yorkshire Post* reported that Yorkshire Seconds had a season with seven finished matches, but that the main object of developing players for the 1st XI was disappointing. The only batsman newcomer,

> who has shown any pretension to county form is Sutcliffe, a 19-year-old right-handed batsman of the Pudsey Britannia club....In Sutcliffe they have a capable right-handed batsman with youth on his side. In his movements on the field he looks every inch a cricketer, and possessing as he does a variety of good strokes, it would seem to be policy to persevere with him.

In 1914 he scored 249 runs averaging 35. His top score was 59.

The British Expeditionary Force would arrive in France today (though official control of the news meant that it was not reported anywhere).

The Times said on 15 August that it too was preparing a history of the war in weekly parts (there were eventually several of these). It also ran a leader on false rumours which could be regarded as a coded notice to the War Office that it might be more forthcoming. Once again the paper planned to print a Sunday special – more precisely three editions. This might be felt to make up for the fact that it contained very little solid news about the war, not reporting the arrival of the BEF in France.

The Daily Express carried a big front-page warning,

> The public are warned against the slightest reliance on the many rumours that are current daily regarding alleged British victories or defeats and the arrival of wounded men or disabled ships in this country. These are, without exception, baseless. The public may be confident that any news of successes or reverses to the British Army will be communicated officially without delay.

Clearly the War Office press team had dropped some hints.

At this stage the War Office, drawing the wrong lessons from the Crimea and South Africa, was determined to keep all information in its own hands and release it as and when it wanted and spun as it wanted. This, of course, meant that it was distrusted and that people listened to rumour and urban myths, whether it was a graphic account of German atrocities or Russians marching through Britain with snow on their boots. But the official news gave no cause for alarm, and so no reason to stop whatever you were doing – including playing cricket.

Five thousand people watched the cricket at Lord's where Surrey advanced to a winning position against Yorkshire, declaring at 549 for 6, Hayes making 134. Yorkshire were bowled out for 204 (Hitch five for 64) and were 33-1 following on. Incidentally Hayward – who was, of course, a professional – was captaining Surrey and would do so for the rest of the season. Cyril Wilkinson, the designated captain, was presumably occupied with war work and the county seems to have run out of possible amateurs although the youngsters Fender and Knight played regularly and Wilkinson captained in the last match against Gloucestershire.

Middlesex came close to equalling Lancashire's first-innings score with 330 against 343. George Hebden, an amateur playing only his second match of the season, made a career-best 101. Lancashire were then 29-1. The wicket at Edgbaston had presumably eased as Kent made the 79 they needed for the loss of only one wicket. Hampshire had a much better second day against Derbyshire, though at 244 Derby were 153 ahead on first innings. Hampshire were 259-7 at stumps, Bowell making 92 and A.C.P.Arnold 52. This had been Alban Arnold's third year at Cambridge, but the first time that he had won his blue. He died in France in July 1916. Worcestershire made short work of Somerset, taking a first-innings lead of 23, bowling them out for 148, and then knocking the runs off without loss.

The *Harrogate Advertiser* said on 15 August, 'Mr H.D.G.Leveson Gower is unable to raise an England XI for the match with Yorkshire arranged to take place at Harrogate starting on 20th.' The game was therefore abandoned. The *Advertiser* did not mention the war here, but it was beginning to be difficult to find amateurs.

MCC issued a statement,

> Owing to the war and inasmuch as every sound man of England will be engaged in some service for his country in her hour of need no cricket will be played at Lord's in September next.

At about this point the General Committee of the Northern Rugby Union considered 'whether the season should be commenced – in view of the present state of affairs due to war.' It was decided that 'no alteration be made in respect of the opening of the season.' The Northern Union, of course, was later to be known as Rugby League, and was by now a 13-a-side fully professional game. In the end the Rugby League championship was played in 1914/15 but then not again until 1919/20.

On 16 August *The Times* ran a four-page Sunday special (with news on the front page!) 'The main fact,' it said, 'is that the German plan of a sudden strike against the French frontier, directed through Belgium, completely miscarried' and there was still no mention of the BEF. The back page was taken up with an advertisement for *The Times History of the War* (weekly at sevenpence).

On the next day there is still no mention of the BEF or that British troops were in France.

Surrey and Middlesex both gained 'brilliant' victories. Surrey bowled out Yorkshire for 315 to win by an innings, while Tarrant beat Lancashire single-handed. The game had looked evenly poised overnight but he took seven for 71 to bowl Lancashire out for 131 and then scored 101 not out in a score of 145-0 for a ten-wicket victory. So the top of the table was unchanged, with Surrey narrowly ahead of Middlesex.

Hampshire, 153 behind on first innings, beat Derbyshire by 15 runs with Newman taking seven for 64.

The top six in the batting averages were all professionals and Colin Blythe now topped the bowling. S.G.Smith, though, was seventh in batting and second in bowling.

Finally on 18 August the papers were able to report that the BEF was in France and advancing to a great battle along the Marne.

Middlesex made 284 against Nottinghamshire (J.W.Hearne 104, Hendren 88) and Nottinghamshire were 82-4. George Pitts, an amateur fast bowler born in Newfoundland, made his Middlesex debut and dismissed George Gunn. This and the next match would constitute his first-class career, though in 1922 he spent about a month in the summer playing for MCC.

6,000 people watched Yorkshire score 386-3 against Sussex, with B.B.Wilson 204* and Rhodes 104*. Ben Wilson played no first-class cricket after the War, though oddly enough he turned out for Taranaki in 1927/28 at nearly 50 years old and indeed made 80 in a first innings of 138 as they lost to the Australians by an innings and 177.

Kent scored 272 against Lancashire in a game that should have been the first in the Dover Week but together with the following one had been transferred to Canterbury as the Crabble ground had been taken over by the military.

Northamptonshire beat Essex and William Wells scored 119 in 95 minutes, his highest score in a first-class career that lasted from 1905 to 1926.

Cricket was resumed at the Oval (prisoners of war having so far failed to arrive) with the Young Amateurs of Surrey meeting the Young Professionals. For the amateurs J.H.Strachan of Charterhouse scored 122. He played only one first-class match – for the Free Foresters in 1926.

On 19 August *The Times* refers to the 'sudden and decidedly unexpected advance of the French into Alsace-Lorraine'. It also reports from a correspondent on the difficulty of obtaining information with reporters being kept well away from the action. The Expeditionary Force, it reports, is being carried by rail to 'certain places'. The Belgian government was moving to Antwerp and was happy it could hold out there for a year. It carried a report of an Alsatian deserter from the German army saying that the Germans were disorganised and starving.

For the first time since the declaration of war *The Times* carried the scores of two matches in full. At Lord's Middlesex, 81 runs ahead on the first innings, were 294-3 in their second, Harry Lee having made 139. His career was in a way advanced by the War. By the start of 1914 he had been on the Middlesex staff since 1906 and had played a few times for the county, but his highest score at this point was 35 not out.

As he tells it[35] he had played at the end of July for MCC against the Gentlemen of Worcestershire and made a hundred. Word got back to Middlesex about this. The county was about to leave for its 'northern tour' to play Yorkshire and Lancashire and was, as has been mentioned earlier, struggling to find a side, so Lee was asked to open the batting and did well enough to play in the Nottinghamshire game.

Lee also talks about having played earlier in the summer for MCC against an army team at Tidworth and 'noticed that several of the army men had books of German grammar with them' and asking why, got a vague answer. The he goes on to remember a conversation with Joe Murrell and J.T.Hearne saying (at some point on the northern tour) that they were pleased that the season had not been cancelled, and that cricket should go on to the end. 'That's all right – if they don't get over here first,' said Joe.

Harry got back to Lord's and P.F.Warner was pushing him to join up,

'Well, young Lee,' he said, 'you look as if you'd make a fine soldier.'
'I don't think so, sir,' I said.
'Aren't you going to join up?' he asked.
'I wasn't thinking of it, sir,' I answered.
He said, 'Hmmm' and walked away.

Joe Murrell said to him, 'you know, everyone'll be joining up, and you won't get much of a show round Lord's if you don't.' Shortly afterwards Harry did enlist. He was shot in the leg in 1915, reported killed, captured, repatriated by the Germans and was told that he would not play cricket again. But he did and played for Middlesex until 1934.

Lancashire went on to 528 against Kent with J.T.Tyldesley making 253. Surrey meanwhile demolished Gloucestershire by an innings and 25, ensuring that they stayed at the top. Hampshire were dominating their game against Somerset, Mead making 158 and reaching 2000 runs for the season.

On 20 August the Germans were reported as advancing towards the Meuse. A report from our boys in France tells of them heading towards battle in a stream of commercial vans requisitioned by the War Office and still bearing their commercial markings. The *Daily Express* quoted a 'high French military authority' who said the war would be over by October.

Racing was to be resumed by the end of the month.

Middlesex beat Nottinghamshire by 239 runs to stay in touch with Surrey. Kent, with a second innings of 422, drew with Lancashire. E.Humphreys made 143 and Frank Woolley 101. Edward Humphreys had been playing for Kent since 1899 and played on for a couple of seasons after the War. Other matches only got summarised scores: Yorkshire beat Sussex by an

---

35   H.W.Lee, *Forty Years of English Cricket*, Clerke & Cockeran, 1948.

innings, Major Booth (normally known to his fellows as William) taking nine wickets in the match. Booth took 141 wickets this year but it was his last: he was to die on the Somme. Hampshire beat Somerset by an innings, H.C.McDonell taking seven for 47 in the second innings, eleven for 104 in the match. Harold McDonell was an amateur leg-spinner who had played for Surrey a few years earlier. He now played for Hampshire, usually turning out in August (the 1911 census shows him as a schoolmaster at Twyford School near Winchester).

Derbyshire bowled Leicestershire out for 56 and went on to win a game they had looked like losing. The captain for this match, Thomas Forrester, took four for 29 and James Horsley, who had switched from Nottinghamshire to Derbyshire (the county of his birth), six for 17. He went on playing for Derbyshire until 1925.

On 21 August the papers reported the death of the Pope, Pius X, later canonised. Father Franz Xavier Wernz, the general of the Jesuit order, had died the day before. *The Times* had a correspondent touring the country, reporting on the state of things: today he was in the Midlands where he found the settled order of life affected only to a limited degree, suggesting that strikes in recent years had caused more disruption.

The Belgian withdrawal from Brussels was explained as being merely tactical.

There was an assurance that racing would resume at Doncaster and Wolverhampton.

There were three county matches in progress and two scores given in full. Kent battered Worcestershire for 461, Woolley 150 not out and S.H.Day 109. Sam Day was an amateur who played until 1919 (by which time he was 41) and had played football for the Corinthians and England. Johnny Tyldesley scored another century as Lancashire totalled 372 against Sussex. In the other match Warwickshire made 288 against Hampshire, F.R.Foster making 92 in an hour and a half.

The Times of 22 August, talking about events after the German capture of Brussels, rhapsodised about 'a glorious country for fighting in, glorious weather and a glorious cause. What soldier could ask for more?' The special correspondent in Boulogne was watching artillery moving towards the front, each hauled by eight horses 'fresh from the English plough' (in some cases not spared so willingly). In fact, battle in earnest was getting very close.

From St Petersburg it was claimed that the Russian army had crossed the Prussian border with half a million men. With increasing enthusiasm the *Daily Express* suggested using the Press Gang to round up 'loafers'.

The *Express* claimed that other papers were spreading rumours that the paper was German-owned and said the Chairman and editor was not and never had been a German, that it was not printed on German paper and that there was not one German on the staff of the *Express*.

In the late news in the *Birmingham Sports Argus* on 22 August there was a release from the wartime Press Bureau:

> In view of the persistent rumours that the notification of casualties have been sent to relatives of men alleged to have been killed, it is officially announced that no such notifications have been dispatched except in the case of those whose names have already been reported in the Press, and that nothing further of any casualties is known at the War Office up to 3.30 pm today.

The *Express* included lengthy previews of the football season, mostly London clubs (including Southern League clubs) and commenting that most had lost players to the war. A lot more space was given to this than the cricket scores.

At Eastbourne Sussex reached 399-9 to take a first-innings lead, A.E.Relf 160 not out. Albert Relf played thirteen Test matches for England and carried on for Sussex until 1921. Hampshire took a first-innings lead of 75 against Warwickshire, reaching 363. They were unlucky at Canterbury, managing only a couple of hours' play (though at Eastbourne and Southampton they played all day) in which Worcestershire moved to 164-5.

County attendances were falling in Kent, and on 22 August the *Kentish Express* said,

> It will be a relief to everyone when this farce called county cricket comes to an end. The people don't want cricket; won't have cricket. Yet it is difficult to decide whether it would be sound policy to stop the games. If all the amusements cease, the country will be more depressed than ever. Yet at present the matches are being played at a great financial loss and the public generally don't want cricket. One reason for playing matches is that their cessation would take away the living of cricket professionals, of a handful of gate officials and prevent the amateurs having a good time at the county club's expense.

On 23 August *The Times* ran a four-page Sunday edition with news on the front page. On 22 August the first serious encounter of the war was beginning as the Germans advanced through Belgium into France. But *The Times* did not see it that way – there were odd indications of German advance but little more.

The Daily Telegraph said that the wisdom of going on with county cricket was clearly shown at Lord's on Saturday, the match between Middlesex and Surrey proving a big attraction to the public. Over 7,000 people were present, 6,125 paying for admission. Middlesex scored 381 with 124 from Patsy Hendren.

'The great battle, said *The Times* on 24 August, 'is beginning at last' in Belgium. What was to become known as the Battle of the Frontiers was to see the first mass slaughter of the war. It also reported that the steady advance of the Russians across East Prussia. It remarks, curiously, that 'our mobilization was unduly delayed' so the BEF had not yet played a part. In fact the battle of Mons had begun on 23 August.

Sunshine after rain at Canterbury had seen Colin Blythe take seven for 20 and Kent beat Worcestershire by an innings and 154 runs. Hampshire beat Warwickshire by four wickets, Arthur Jaques taking seven for 51 and reaching 100 for the season. Sussex beat Lancashire by six wickets, Jupp and Vincett bowling unchanged to dismiss Lancashire for 146. Essex scored 318 on the first day of their match against Northamptonshire with G.M.Louden, batting at Number 10, making 64. George Louden was one of those amateurs called on from time to time by Essex (like the other poorer counties). He was not a graduate and in 1911 had still been living at home and working as a stockbroker's clerk. Leicestershire made 233 against Nottinghamshire. Fred Barratt took eight for 75 as he reached 100 wickets in his first season.

The short list of leading averages showed three batsmen – Hobbs, Mead and Woolley – past 2000 runs.

On 25 August it was reported that Namur had fallen to the Germans: British forces had been holding on at Mons since Sunday afternoon, casualties were reported not to be heavy. The French were falling back, having inflicted tremendous losses on the Germans. Even *The Times* admitted that this was a day of bad news. But 'our ultimate success is certain.'

At Lord's Surrey were out for 206 (Hobbs 56, Ducat 55 not out) but Middlesex chose not to enforce the follow-on and reached 135-4 in their second innings. *The Times* reports 10,000 watching (on a weekday).

Warwickshire and Kent got two innings in on the first day at Gravesend: Kent 167, Warwickshire 179. Hardinge was ill and was replaced in the Kent side by G.V.E.Whitehead, still at school at Clifton. George Whitehead, after playing only two first-class matches, was killed in action in October 1918.

Gloucestershire had a poor first day against Yorkshire at Bristol, all out for 94 against Booth and Drake. Yorkshire then reached 256-5 by the close with Roy Kilner undefeated on 101. For Hampshire against Lancashire at Bournemouth, Horace Bowell was 194 not out of 365-9: he went on the next day to 204, his highest score.

On 26 August it was reported that the BEF, a small but professional army among huge conscript armies, was falling back at Mons as part of a general retreat, but apparently in good order: there was talk of 2,000 casualties 'hors de combat'. Lord Kitchener had made a statement in the House of Lords, suggesting a managed retreat without massive losses. The knowledge that British forces had been engaged, that there were casualties and that they had been forced to retreat, however this was spun by the War Office, marked a change in public attitudes. This was going to be a serious business after all. Until then you could almost pretend that it was 'business as usual'. After that there was some unease about the idea of enjoying yourself.

The Middlesex-Surrey game at Lord's was drawn. Middlesex went on to 215-6 before declaring and Surrey were not going to chase 391 in 280 minutes. They made 252-6 before the game came to an end.

Warwickshire v Kent ended in two days with Warwickshire bowled out by Fielder and Woolley for 99. Yorkshire beat Gloucestershire by an innings and 227, Kilner going on to 169 of Yorkshire's 405. Booth (twelve for 89) and Drake (eight for 81) bowled unchanged through both innings, dismissing Gloucestershire for 84 in the second innings. At Bournemouth Lancashire made 389 for a narrow first-innings lead, J.S.Heap 132 not out, his only first-class hundred in a career which lasted from 1903 to 1921. For Essex against Northamptonshire two amateurs made hundreds: C.D.McIver 118 and Geoffrey Davies 100 in his last game.

After the game the Essex committee met in the pavilion and agreed that 'Members of the Staff volunteering in the war should have their places kept open for them.' This was not entirely a matter of doddery old buffers blithely sending young men to their deaths: three of the committee – Douglas, McIver and Charles Round – soon joined up and were commissioned in the Army. Round was the only son of the club's founder James and captain of the 2nd XI, although he played no more cricket in 1914. Away in Belgium, a 16-year-old boy called John Parr, who had falsified his age, had already become the first British soldier to be killed. War was casting an increasingly long shadow over the whole country, including its cricketers.

Lord Kitchener had 'practically' got his first 100,000 men: but more were needed. On 28 August a new recruiting advertisement appeared. Kitchener was advertising for another 100,000 men – the age limit was now 35 but ex-soldiers up to 45 and some ex-NCOs up to 50 could apply. The minimum height was 5'3", chest 34".

The *Western Daily Press's* regular columnist 'North Somerset' chuntered that last Saturday he was in the garden and 'what did I see but a huge brake laden with strong young men in flannels and their friends all come out into the country to play a return cricket match and thus induce a similar number of country chaps to waste half a day that could well have been spent in helping the old folk with their gardens at home.'

The Times war update started,

> Our thoughts are with our gallant Army. If we do not at all discuss its fortunes and speculate upon its future it is because its deeds and its sufferings are not revealed to us. We are kept completely in the dark regarding the recent action at Mons.

The Times was especially peeved because other countries seemed much more ready to say what was going on, while there was not even any official announcement about what had happened since the apparently orderly retreat from Mons, and no indication of casualties. Questions were asked in the House of Commons and batted away. But if people could not be trusted with the truth they were going to listen to rumour, and with wounded soldiers returning they could hardly be silenced.

The paper also editorialised on the dropping of bombs on Antwerp by a Zeppelin: a new horror of war. Was it a breach of the Hague Convention?

The only cricket had been the last day of Hampshire v Lancashire and that was spoiled by rain so the game was left drawn. WG's famous letter had been published in *The Sportsman* on this day. Why did he write to *The Sportsman*? At least a probable answer is that WG may have read *The Sportsman* but not *The Times*: another possibility that the letter was intended for the professionals as the amateurs (who might have been *Times* readers) were already doing their bit. He wrote,

> There are many cricketers who are already doing their duty, but there are many more who do not seem to realise that in all probability they will have to serve either at home or abroad before the war is brought to a conclusion. The fighting on the Continent is very severe and will probably be prolonged. I think the time has arrived when the county cricket season should be closed, for it is not fitting at a time like the present that able-bodied men should play day after day and pleasure-seekers look on. There are many who are young and able and yet are hanging back. I should like to see all first-class cricketers of a suitable age etc. set a good example and come to the help of their country without delay in its hour of need.

There is a kind of popular belief that this letter was crucial, but there seems to be no such contemporary judgement. It is not mentioned in the newspapers and, of course, the next round of matches in the Championship went ahead.

The Surrey committee met at this point and decided to abandon their two remaining matches against Sussex and Leicestershire. But they were the only county games scheduled anywhere for September and that was the only change in the championship fixture list.

The allies had 'retired' to a line between Le Cateau and Cambrai. As to how this had happened the authorities were silent. The first wounded had arrived at Folkestone but there was very little about what they said. The Russians were 'sweeping on' though in fact they were locked with the Germans at the battle of Tannenberg which would change the direction of the war in the east.

Middlesex were playing Kent at Lord's: it was the last match scheduled there for the season and also Middlesex's last fixture. Middlesex made 205 of which J.W.Hearne scored 110 not out. Kent were 96-7 at the close.

Warwickshire made 177 against Surrey (F.R.Foster 81, W.G.Quaife 60, Rushby six for 65) and Surrey were 70-4.

Somerset bowled Yorkshire out for 162 at Weston-super-Mare J.J.Bridges five for 59 : Bridges had been a Somerset professional since 1911, but was to play on after the war as an amateur. Somerset then collapsed for 44, Booth (five for 27) and Drake (five for 16) bowling unchanged, though this was not unduly onerous as the innings only lasted 15 overs.

Essex made 162 against Hampshire at Bournemouth; the home side were 137-2 at the close.

On 29 August *The Times* was rightly horrified by the German destruction of Louvain and particularly the burning of the university library. This was not how war had been fought (if you ignored what might have been done by European countries – even gallant little Belgium – outside Europe). There had been a naval encounter off Heligoland, claimed as a brilliant victory, which was something of an exaggeration.

Blackheath Rugby Club had decided to cancel its fixtures for the season.

Middlesex had ended their season by beating Kent. Set 366 to win, Kent were all out for 67. Rambler in the *Daily Mirror* disapproved, 'And there is another ignoble band of whom I caught a fleeting glimpse in St John's Wood yesterday. They were the noble patriots pouring into Lord's to cheer on the great contest between Kent and Middlesex,' quoting 'a man' as calling them 'rabbit-faced pinheads' and suggesting 'a young man who can spend his time at a cricket match just now would assuredly run at the sight of a German.' The *Mirror* did not generally provide massive coverage for cricket, giving merely summarised scores of the first-class games.

Yorkshire beat Somerset, who managed 90 in their second innings. Alonzo Drake took all ten for 35 in 8.5 overs – fifteen for 51 in the match. This was the first first-class game to be played at Clarence Park, Weston-super-Mare. According to A.W.Pullin [36], 'the wicket had been crudely prepared by a local clergyman whose zeal was unmistakeable, but who lacked expertise in the wicket-maker's craft. A merest glance at the pitch was sufficient to make one realise that trouble for batsmen lay ahead.'

Dr Arthur Littlejohn, who had played a few matches for Middlesex in May and June, found himself second in the national batting averages and fourth in the bowling – both placings were a trifle anomalous, since apart from taking six for 42 against Worcestershire in May he had done little bowling and he had only batted five times (two of them not out) with a highest score of 66*.

Sunday was 30 August and there is no copy of that day's paper in *The Times* archive, though the edition was highly controversial. This was an issue in which The Times printed a despatch from Amiens that gave a rather more accurate view than official statements: it was over-excitedly characterised in the Commons as saying 'that the Army had met with disaster, and that British regiments had been broken to bits.'

On this day Lord Roberts had made a speech while inspecting the new 7th battalion of the City of London Regiment, saying,

> My feeling towards you is one of intense admiration. How very different is your action to that of the men who can still go with their cricket and football, as if the very existence of the country were not at stake. This is not the time to play games, wholesome as they are in the piping days of peace.

No room here for the Francis Drake approach. Lord Roberts' speech was

---

36   A.W.Pullin, *History of Yorkshire County Cricket 1903-1923*, Chorley and Pickersgill.

reported everywhere, but could not affect the first-class programme as that was finishing.

There was a strange general impression that the BEF had been magnificent, but that we were allowed to know very little about it. *The Times* talked of 5000 to 6000 casualties. *The Daily Express* called it, 'The most brilliant deed in British history.'

MCC announced the cancellation of the Scarborough Festival, 'it being evident that the continuation of first-class cricket is hurtful to the feelings of a section of the public.'

The FA was meeting to consider its position. Rugby teams were packing up, though the Cumberland RFU suggested that they should carry on for the time being.

Surrey were beaten at Edgbaston; wanting 211, they collapsed for 130, F.R.Foster five for 48: they were, however, still top of the table, though the *Daily Express* pointed out that, 'there is a chance that Surrey will not win the title after all. In losing to Warks their percentage was reduced 73.33 and Middlesex, having completed their season, have a percentage of 70%.' Surrey needed seven points from their last three matches although, of course, they had cancelled two of them.

Hampshire beat Essex by an innings and 19 runs. At Old Trafford Lancashire were 299-3, J.T.Tyldesley 122 not out, in reply to 339. M.K.Foster made 158 for Worcestershire against Derbyshire: one of the seven brothers this was his highest first-class score though he stayed on to captain the county from 1923 to 1925. In that match came the debut for Worcestershire of John Harber from Norton. According to the *Evening Despatch* he had gone for a trial on the Saturday and was immediately put in the team having only played village cricket. It was his only first-class match and *CricketArchive* has no further trace of him as a cricketer at any level. He took three wickets at reasonable cost, but it was Worcestershire's last Championship match until 1920. In 1911 he had been living and working on his father's farm at Earls Croome and he died in 1962 at Baughton Hill Farm, Earls Croome, so he must have gone back to the land and worked there for the rest of his life.

Lancashire v Northamptonshire was drawn. The 17-year-old S.T. (Thomas) Askham was playing for Northamptonshire, his fifth game of the month. He was still at Wellingborough School, where he was regarded as exceptionally promising. He left after 1915 and, another young Second Lieutenant, was killed in action in August 1916.

On 1 September the *Daily Express* says that 'Berlin is in a state of panic' with the Russians advancing.

The football season started today and the Football Association said that the game would continue and the War Office was in favour. The 1914/15 season was played out but the Football League was suspended for the duration after that.

A full-page advert from Eastbourne proclaimed that all was normal, including steamer excursions.

On 2 September the first official details of British losses had been released. The absurdity of the official clampdown on news is shown by the *Daily Express* carrying an article about new German guns of amazing range and power written not by an expert or even a reporter but by the Vicar of Gorleston who had the story from a wounded French officer.

Surrey finished with a win by an innings and 36 runs against Gloucestershire which would have been much more but for an innings of 165 in 120 minutes by the captain, C.O.H.Sewell, South African-born and the county secretary as well as captain. Gloucestershire, who had a dismal record for the season (one victory and 17 defeats in their 22 matches), only had ten men for this game as Alf Dipper had already enlisted. Essex beat Somerset, Nottinghamshire beat Leicestershire heavily. In that game William Odell was playing his last match for Leicestershire. He died at Passchendaele. At Bournemouth Hampshire scored 477 for a lead of 228 against Kent (Mead 128) while at Hove Sussex were 316-1 (Vine 164* and Jupp 108*) in reply to Yorkshire's 461.

Mr C.B.Fry had been gazetted as an honorary lieutenant in the RNR (though he was not going to see action – he was involved with the *TS Mercury*). Harrods was sending 20,000 one-ounce packets of tobacco to the front. It was reported that at Deal several young women went round fixing white goose feathers in coat lapels and hatbands of young men lounging around the front. Admiral Charles Fitzgerald had founded the Order of the White Feather, encouraging young women to hand out white feathers to young men not in uniform. It was discouraged by the authorities (since many of the victims might be convalescent soldiers or engaged in war work) but lived long in legend.

The Times reported a rush to enlist in London, with over 4,000 men joining up. The military correspondent explained that the object of the war in France was to tie down as many German troops as possible so allowing the Russians to deliver the knockout blow (though in reality the Russians had been defeated at Tannenberg and from now onwards would be going backwards). The paper did report heavy Russian losses but morale uninjured. St Petersburg was to be renamed Petrograd because it removed the German 'burg' from the name.

From Paris stories included a flood of refugees, new atrocity stories (in this case almost certainly false) and the information that the Germans were starving and reduced to eating their horses.

By 3 September *The Times* is admitting to heavy losses for the BEF, though far fewer than those suffered by the French and Belgians or, so it is claimed, the Germans.

Hampshire beat Kent by an innings, Jaques, Kennedy and McDonell bowling them out for 145. The last act was at Hove where Sussex and Yorkshire gave up the game as a draw at tea time. Sussex were dismissed for 405.

Giving Yorkshire a lead of 56. In their second innings Yorkshire reached 123-5 when Rhodes was caught by Street off the bowling of Vincett; his partner Hirst was left undefeated with 18. A.W.Pullin later wrote,

> the seriousness of the war had been brought home to everybody by this time. When the players were assembling for their game at Brighton (sic), I had a conversation with Major Booth and Roy Kilner, and they told me that they had decided to enlist directly they returned home.[37]

Oddly enough, the last game to finish in 1939 was also between Sussex and Yorkshire at Hove.

The Times announced that 'all the counties had now completed their fixtures for the season.' Surrey had cancelled their last two matches, one of which was at the Oval against Leicestershire and might have been a problem and the Scarborough Festival had been cancelled, but that was all. The paper had published nothing about future intentions.

The final championship table was published, showing Surrey as champions, Middlesex second, followed by Kent, Yorkshire and Hampshire (Hampshire's best-ever finish at that point). *The Newcastle Journal*, on the other hand, said on 7 September that,

> Probably to everyone's relief, the cricket season is at an end, the County Championship being won by Surrey, though the confirmation of the MCC is, under the special circumstances, necessary before the title is bestowed.

They did not actually make that decision until November.

First-class cricket might be over, but the war carried on. On 4 September *The Times* still says, 'the military situation in France is not very easy to define from any published information': it still talks of a great Russian victory against Austria-Hungary. So far there had been 260,000 volunteers.

On 5 September, remarkably enough given its financial position, the Worcestershire club had placed an advert in the *Sports Argus* for young cricketers (preferably bowlers) who might want to join the staff for the next season.

Football had started and cricket disappeared almost entirely from the *Daily Express* before the end of the season.

On 7 September under the heading 'Patriotism before Sport,' *The Times* lists eight Hampshire professionals who had joined the 5th Hampshire Territorials. It also lists eleven Hampshire amateurs either on active service or accepted for service.

Outside the first-class game cricket carried on. On 10 September the *Newcastle Chronicle* published a table for the East Tyne League (some had games to play) and announced for Saturday the final of the Durham Senior Cup between Westland (Sunderland) and New Brancepeth. As late as 20

---

37 A.W.Pullin, History of Yorkshire Cricket 1903 to 1923, Chorley & Pickersgill, 1923

September *The Observer* was still publishing a long list of club fixtures.

On 29 September the *Manchester Guardian* printed the averages for the Manchester Club; many of the Lancashire players had turned out during the season.

If Worcestershire was the most obvious financial basket case, some of the other counties were not doing much better. On 22 October the Gloucestershire committee was recommending to a special meeting not to wind up the club, but to keep plugging away. However only one match in the season had attracted enough support to pay its way and it was proposed not to pay the professionals.

In October a general meeting of Somerset members had been told that there were substantial financial problems and that if cricket were to be played in 1915 they would have to drop fixtures with Yorkshire and Lancashire away to save money, and that if their debenture holders foreclosed, the club would go out of existence. They had needed a guarantee of £500 to carry on in 1914, but the outbreak of war had destroyed the hope of making money at the Taunton Festival.

Lancashire had a meeting in October too and had had a very poor season, having lost over £1300. The position here was secure and there were decent crowds until nearly the end of the season, but it was not good news.

To some extent the war saved the county clubs: most of the members continued to pay their subscriptions and there were no substantial expenses.

Where Essex were concerned, by the end of September 1914, 'all available members of the team (amateur and professional) and of the ground staff had already joined the army.' At first five members of the groundstaff were retained with no alteration in wages, but it was soon obvious that the war would not be over by Christmas and on 14 December the committee 'agreed that notice be given to A.C.Russell, J.Freeman, and B.Tremlin that the committee did not see their way to employ them after December 31st.' Only the head groundsman, E.C.Freeman, and his assistant Walter 'Bung' Brewer stayed on, both being beyond military age. Theirs was no sinecure, for the ground was used throughout the war for a variety of events intended to raise morale. In 1919 'all county cricketers who had served in the war' were invited to the club's annual dinner as guests, and the annual report noted that during the war 'no professionals were engaged and no one eligible for military service was employed on the ground.'

Giles Phillips writes in *On Fenner's Sward*[38],

> On 27th October 1914, all members of the University eleven were reported to be absent from Cambridge on military duty, and arrangements for matches were in abeyance. As a result of the lack of matches, or any other activities, subscriptions were reduced from

38   Giles Phillips, *on Fenner's Sward,* History Press, 2005

£1 1s to 7/6 and at the end of 1915.... The appointments of captain, secretary and assistant treasurer were indefinitely postponed... the only action seen at the ground during this hiatus was of the military variety, including sports like officers' races run in full uniform.

Chapter Eight
Minor Counties

Minor County cricket had been hit hard and earlier than the first-class game. Although the clubs needed organisation like the first-class game and were organised as members' clubs in the same way, the players were nearly all amateurs and teams would have been early affected by players and indeed administrators joining up (or simply unable to arrange their affairs to play).

The *Sports Argus* carried an article about Staffordshire's season which had ended with an average of 86%, but the county had to cancel their last two matches, against Norfolk and Surrey II, because of the war. 21 Minor County matches altogether had been cancelled. Staffordshire had 12 fixtures but of the ten which they played they won eight and lost only one, so they clearly topped the table but were not immediately declared champions, the title only being formally awarded when Hertfordshire decided not to seek a challenge match. Staffordshire had, of course, the advantage of the incomparable Sydney Barnes. Despite missing a number of matches through injury or league commitments, Barnes took 48 wickets at an average of 6.18 (and 85 at 5.10 in his league engagement with Porthill); and he was the dominant bowler for the Players against the Gentlemen in his only first-class match of the summer.

Berkshire played Dorset at Reading on 3 and 4 August and started another against Cornwall on 7 August, also at Reading. This was left unfinished on 7 August, but that was purely because of weather. The newspaper reports of these two matches make no reference whatsoever to any disruption to the teams, or to the matches themselves, arising specifically from the outbreak of war but the *Berkshire Chronicle* report of 7 August included this statement: 'both sides were unable to place their best teams in the field, there being a number of notable absentees on the Berkshire side.' Unfortunately no names are given of these absentees, nor – more significantly for the present project – were any explanations given as to the reasons for their absence. They could have been war-related or it could have been that the players concerned preferred to spend their August Bank Holiday elsewhere, or were injured, or ....

The next scheduled Minor Counties matches were both in Reading – against Buckinghamshire on 10 August, and two days later against Devon. Both of these matches were casualties of the war, as were Berkshire's two remaining fixtures against Dorset at Sherborne on 21 August and Buckinghamshire at Slough on 24 August.

The circumstances of the abandonment of the county's fixtures, and particularly the first Buckinghamshire game, were described in the *Reading Observer* on 15 August as follows,

> Berkshire has finished its matches for the present season ... On Friday last [7 August] the Bucks team wired enquiring whether they were expected, and Sir Charles Y. Nepean [the Berkshire captain from 1903 to 1914] replied in the affirmative. On Saturday morning, however, another telegram was received saying the Bucks team regretted having to scratch owing to nine men of the team having been picked for the front. Berkshire have also lost eight or nine of their players, and in consequence no more matches will be played this year. The break-up of the 'Reading Week' [the two consecutive matches scheduled at Reading for 10 and 12 August] will no doubt adversely affect the finances.

For Norfolk, in terms of cricketing activity, the month of July 1914 was no different from that of any other July. The county club played the bulk of its away matches in the Minor Counties Championship – comfortably beating Bedfordshire, but having to struggle to avoid defeat against Hertfordshire and Staffordshire – so that early August was left clear for the county's home matches to constitute the 34th Norfolk Festival.

Surrey II met Essex II at the Oval on 26 and 27 August: Surrey should have played Wiltshire on the two previous days but this was cancelled.

Hertfordshire played Cambridgeshire at Hitchin on 21 and 22 August and then Bedfordshire on 24 and 25 August. Cambridgeshire played Norfolk – these are played between neighbours. Most of the minor county matches from mid-August were cancelled, the first being Dorset v Buckinghamshire on 7 and 8 August. County second XIs found it easier, but then they were based on young professionals and they shared the first-class infrastructure.

It was reported that Northumberland had cancelled fixtures with Lincolnshire and Cheshire because of the difficulty in raising a side because of members being mobilised.

Lincolnshire v Durham which should have started on 12 August at Grantham was abandoned as the military authorities had taken over the ground.

The Essex II game against Glamorgan due to be played on 20 and 21 August was abandoned because of the war – presumably at Glamorgan's request, since Essex hastily arranged a replacement Club and Ground match against the touring Merion CC at Leyton on 19 and 20 August. The Essex side for this game was decidedly a scratch one – most of the team were not even 2nd XI regulars.

By the time of the last match against Surrey II at the Oval on 26 and 27 August, Charles Round and several of the older men had already enlisted, so Essex fielded a very young team.

29 July was the first day of a two-day friendly which Glamorgan had organised at The Gnoll in Neath against a combined Briton Ferry XI largely as a means of thanking the Town and Steelworks clubs for their help

in releasing players for Minor County matches, and also as a means of helping to raise funds for the two organisations. The match also promised to give some decent practice to the county's players ahead of the next batch of scheduled games in the Minor County Championship, but with talk of impending invasion by German troops, several of the amateurs who worked in the Cardiff area and had initially agreed to turn out for Glamorgan were now unable to take time off from their jobs as their employers started to make contingency plans for the country going to war.

The upshot was that several of those from the Cardiff area who had previously agreed to play at Briton Ferry dropped out on the day before the match and although replacements were sought, another player withdrew on the morning of the game, so Glamorgan turned up with only ten men, chiefly from the Swansea and Neath clubs. Harry Creber was in fine form with the ball and the Swansea spinner duly led the Glamorgan XI to a 50-run victory over the combined side.

Glamorgan's matches on 17 and 18 August against Wiltshire at Trowbridge and Essex II at Leyton on 19 and 20 August were cancelled.

There was to be no Minor County Championship in 1919 and Monmouthshire did not re-enter until 1921.

Chapter Nine
Recreational Cricket

In 1914 cricket was played at some level by a large part of the male population, and the interruption of that was as melancholy as any of the war's privations. In *Memoirs of a Fox-hunting Man* Siegfried Sassoon recalled the end of the season, 'I thought of that last cricket match, on August Bank Holiday, when I was at Hoadley Rectory playing for the Rector's XI against the village .... Parson Colwood had three sons in the service, and his face showed it.'

Long before that, however, (and by August it must have seemed a very long time before) the season started normally enough. It will have started a little earlier than the first-class season: the *Chelmsford Chronicle* (a weekly) was reporting local scores by its 1 May issue.

First-class cricketers were likely to be newspaper readers because they had the time, especially when playing away from home and staying in hotels or bed and breakfast accommodation. Until almost the end of July what most local cricketers knew or wanted to know about the rest of the world would have depended on what they did for a living.

There are a number of factors which might have brought local cricket to a halt some time in August. Men had enlisted, and the captain or the effective sponsor or the secretary might have been recalled to his regiment. Cricket fields might have become unavailable, wanted by the military or ultimately going under the plough.

Transport to matches at any distance could have become difficult as motor vehicles and horses were requisitioned for the war effort. Local opinion might be unfavourable (the local vicar might preach against you carrying on). Against that was a feeling in many circles that the real offence was spectators enjoying themselves, and that did not really apply at the local level.

In many cases the local papers do not give an unambiguous answer. Reported matches peter out in late August or early September but it is hard to say whether that was because games were not played (and if so whether because of the war or the weather) or because the papers had no space to report them because they were full of war news or publishing smaller editions (as the county reports were truncated by *The Times*).

The *Harrow Observer*, too, had an editorial at the beginning of September suggesting that young men who play football, cricket and other games (or watch or read about them) should realise that they now had better things to do. It was, of course, the case that a fair few regular cricketers were not in a position to enlist (the original upper limit after all was 30 and married men were not being taken).

The last match to be found in Harrow was a match played on 5 September between Harrow Derelicts and Harrow Wesleyans (!). This was the only match reported in the 11 September issue of the *Harrow Observer*.

The *Oxford Times* took a decidedly different view on 15 August,

> I wish to make a strong appeal to those cricketers and outdoor sportsmen who are not engaged directly or indirectly, in military operations. It is to continue to indulge in their favourite pastime and so occupy to the best advantage their time. While any hilarity or excitement is to be deprecated, there can be no harm in a game of cricket, golf, tennis, etc. provided the main reason is to get healthy exercise. For this reason I, like many others, regret the precipitate action of the Airey Cup[39] committee in abandoning their competition for the season. It would have been far better to have played the matches as friendlies, charged a gate, and to give a percentage of the takings to the Mayor's Relief Fund. In this way cricketers could have done something for their colleagues who have gone to the front and the dependants they have left behind, besides indulging in a game warranted to keep them fit for any call that might be made on them later.
>
> It is essential that we should continue our daily routine as if nothing was happening. This is the best way to help, and is far better than prejudicing our unoccupied time by prohibiting games. Of course if it can be shown that outdoor sportsmen can help their country in any other way, I am sure the suggestion has only to be made and cricketers etc. will immediately respond to the call. There is no greater patriot than the sportsman when the necessity arises.

This was followed by quoting similar opinions from *Athletic News* and *The Sportsman*, and the message was reinforced the following week,

> I have been both surprised and delighted during this week to find the number of gentlemen of standing in the City who disapprove of the action of those misguided and selfish individuals, who tried to stop all sports, on the ground that they were invidious during the stirring times through which we are passing. When young men are not involved in war duties, they are continuing their games, and so occupying their spare time in the best possible way. In this crisis they have shown more sense than those who profess to be their leaders.

This was 22 August. On 29 August it was reported that league clubs in the Oxford area were trying to finish their fixtures and a week later that they had done so. There were unfinished games but they did not affect the leading positions.

On 19 September in Oxfordshire a list of local cricketers who had enlisted

---

39 The Airey Cup (established in 1890) continues to this day as a knockout competition for local clubs.

was published. This was done by team, even splitting out the 1st XI players from 2nd XI ones to demonstrate how many of each XI had gone to war. The suggestion was also made to clubs that their end of season awards for batting and bowling should not be given and that money should be sent to one of the local war funds instead.

Of course by August the public schools and the universities had finished their fixtures for the season (the schools were to carry on throughout the war). Country-house parties – if there still were any – after the 'glorious twelfth' and the start of grouse-shooting would, by this time in the year, be shooting rather than playing cricket.

The structure of the game was well established. Local cricket leagues were established throughout the country and if you had a league going you had an extra motive to finish the season.

Stephen Baldwin has researched the story of Leamington Cricket Club as an example. This was the sort of club that did not play league cricket. There were barracks at nearby Budbrooke, and the club had large numbers of officers among its membership. Stephen writes,

> Membership records for the late nineteenth century list Generals Dandridge, Raft and Thorneycroft, Lieutenant-Generals Keir and Prinsep and Brigadier Generals Collins and Wiggen. Following them in rank were three colonels, three majors and three captains. There is little evidence of most of these officers having played much cricket, but their presence as social members would have done much for the prestige of the nascent club. No doubt they were, on occasions, useful in adjusting the duties of other ranks to make them available to play, especially those who were able to 'help with the bowling'.

From the middle of August the 1914 season shuddered to a halt. Leamington CC would not play again until 1920, although the Club remained open 'administratively'. But the bad news was quick to arrive. In October Sir Francis Waller was killed in action. Not only had Sir Francis been the club's President for many years but he was, through the Woodcote estate, its landlord: his loss would have serious consequences for the Club.

Because the Club was 'administratively open' it held an AGM in 1915, at which the temporary honorary secretary, W.J.P.Whitsed, proudly reported that 35 members of the Club had joined His Majesty's Forces. In the record of the meeting he wrote,

> This is a record of which the club has every right to be proud and the Committee confidently appeal to all the Members at home to do their best to keep the club going, so that when those at present doing their bit for King and Country return they will be able to enjoy their cricket as before

The meeting also reports a deficit of £42 3s 7d, a portent of difficulties ahead. Whitsed was temporary honorary secretary because the substantive post holder was in France. Samuel Sandford Forsyth had been the hard-working club secretary in the years running up to the outbreak of war, but had been one of the first to volunteer. On 25 September 1915 he was killed in action.

The club recovered and was playing again by 1920.

Turning to Kent, on Saturday 1 August the *Herne Bay Press* was reporting normally on two of Herne Bay's games against Gillingham and Whitstable Westmeads. It also reported – on the front page – two meetings of the non-militant wing of the Suffrage movement. There was no mention of international events. By Saturday 8 August the front page was devoted to the war and its consequences as it spoke of the 'shadow of war over the holidays.' It quoted at length (still on the front page) the sermons delivered by various clergymen, C of E and nonconformist. Even the Catholic Church got a brief mention. Remarkably enough, it did the same the following Saturday. The Herne Bay Gas and Electricity Company saw an opportunity to suggest that people 'stock their cellars with coke'. The *Herne Bay Press* reported Herne Bay's matches. The Town Clerk of Margate said it was not true that civilians had been ordered off the seafront.

Be that as it may, the *Dartford Chronicle* on Friday 7 August was showing a full fixture list for local cricket – 13 games on the Saturday and two midweek games. The same was true for the editions of the 14 and the 21, though the 28 August edition only carried one match report suggesting that not all these games were played. The 4 September edition listed nine fixtures for the following day, but neither this nor later editions carried any scores or match reports.

On 15 August the *Herne Bay Press* reported that a farmer had been shot and injured by a supposed German spy. At 3.45 am (getting ready for work) Mr Taylor had been accosted 'in guttural accents by a man of decided Teutonic appearance'.

A main interest for the Kent papers was on the condition of the hops. Flower shows were everywhere before the end of August.

The *Kentish Express* opined on 15 August,

> We are in a state of War and economy must be exercised in everything. Hence, the reduced size of the paper this week. Consumers have agreed to husband the resources of the country and to prevent a famine later on are already bring out their papers in smaller size.

It was reported that,

> The Ashford Beaver Cricket Club are patriotic. Eleven of the number are now serving their country, comprising three Reserves, six Territorials and two Policemen. Needless to say the club's remaining fixtures have been cancelled.

Ramsgate St George's cricket tour of West Kent (Tonbridge, Southborough etc...) was abandoned as soon as war was declared, having played three matches.

The Mote Cricket Week at Maidstone was abandoned. It seems that here there were more early cancellations. Because of its proximity to the Channel coast Kent may have been more affected by logistical problems than most areas.

In Berkshire minor cricket, the Reading & District League programme was completed, with an extra play-off match to decide the championship contested on 29 August. Some club games were called off during August, but either the newspapers are silent as to the reason, or else it is made clear it was a result of bad weather – Saturday 8 August was a particularly wet day in that part of the world.

The war very nearly had a major impact on the outcome of the Reading & District League. At the start of August, Wokingham London Road were heading Division 1 of the competition and were unbeaten, and 'it was all Lombard-street to a china orange' [*Reading Observer*, 29 August] that they would win the title. In mid-August they were in the position that they would win the championship so long as they did not lose both their last two matches, but lose them they did. *The Reading Observer* commented on 29 August,

> the calling up of Riddle and Whittingham by the military authorities proved disastrous, for the team fell to pieces, and successive defeats by Stoke Row (at home) and by Palmer Club (away) followed.

A week earlier, in reporting the loss to Stoke Row which was the Wokingham club's first home defeat in five years, the *Reading Observer* had referred to the absent Riddle and Whittingham as 'their two clever bowlers, who are away with the 'Terriers'.'

The heavy defeat by the Palmer Club (WLR 121, PC 126-1) meant that those two teams ended the season with identical records, and a play-off was arranged to decide the championship. Wokingham London Road won this match 'contrary to expectations', scoring 137 and then bowling out Palmer Club for 71. So in the end the war did not affect the destination of the league title – but it had very much looked as though it would.

Keith Walmsley has compared these two sides' teams in the play-off with their sides in their league games played on 4 July (a pre-war date chosen at random). It turns out that eight of the WLR side played in both matches, as against only seven for the Palmer Club. Riddle and Whittingham apart, there is no evidence as to why particular players were missing from the later match. But, if nothing else, this extremely small sample suggests that top-level local club cricket was not hugely disrupted by the outbreak of war, even if some individuals became unavailable for selection from early August.

By early September a number of clubs in Berkshire were cancelling fixtures 'for the duration' – or at least, until the end of the 1914 season. Thus the *Reading Mercury* of 5 September reports that Easthampstead and Hurst clubs had abandoned their remaining fixtures: 'Owing to the war the Easthampstead Cricket Club have abandoned their matches for the rest of the season'.....'The Hurst Club did not fulfil their engagement on Saturday [29 August], as owing to the present crisis it has been decided to abandon the last fixtures.'

The *Reading Mercury's* brief report of the match on 29 August between Streatley and Headington Hill Hall includes this,

> During the interval (between innings) the two teams sat down to tea.... Mr W.S.Rawson took the opportunity of saying a few words on the present crisis, and made it known that no more matches would be played by the (Streatley) club, as it was not a time for games. He appealed strongly to those of an enlistable age to come forward at once and give their services for the defence of their country.

In a long feature in the *Berkshire Chronicle* of 11 September, headed 'The war and sport – Are games to continues? – What Reading people think'. The feature gives the views of half a dozen Reading 'worthies' (not man-in-the-street vox pops, despite the headline), almost all of whom discussed the issue solely in terms of football. There is no mention of cricket in the entire article, apart from a reference quoted from a sermon given by the Rev R. Gordon Fairbairn at the King's Road Baptist Chapel [no date given - maybe on Sunday 6 September); 'Upon the subject of sport, we must be careful not to select one particular branch, such as football or cricket, while we still participate in our rounds at golf and our quiet rubber at whist.'

There was a lot of cricket in Sussex. Horsham and its attendant villages have a long tradition of cricket. In 1914 virtually all of these villages had a cricket team.

Coverage of the war came late to Horsham. There was virtually no mention of it at all in the *West Sussex County Times* prior to Saturday 8 August but then considerable column inches were devoted to it each week. Just outside the town stands Christ's Hospital School which had only relocated there in 1901. On 6 August the school buildings were commandeered by the military authorities as a detention centre for German nationals and prisoners of war. Before long there would be 500 Germans quartered there.

Within days the impact of the war was being experienced by local industry and commerce as reservists, Territorials and volunteers left civilian employment to join their units. The loss of 20 men from the local postal services resulted in deliveries being reduced from four to three per day.

Up until 8 August there was little change to the volume of local cricket matches being reported, but then it virtually dropped off a cliff. The difficulty is in establishing whether, as their players began to enlist, teams stopped playing – or kept on playing in a lesser key but felt it was somehow unpatriotic to report them. Clues are slight, but the suspicion is that it was primarily (but not exclusively) the former.

In the 15 August edition, there were no match reports but we know that Horsham CC drew with Pirates CC on Monday 10 and played out another draw with Mr G.N.Dickens' XI on Thursday 13. Then there followed a note advising that the remaining fixture of the Horsham Cricket Club had been cancelled owing to the war. The town ground was still being used, however.

On 20 August Horsham YMCA (a well-known local side) beat the Wasps, while as late as 29 August the Junior Conservatives played Roffey CC (both well-known local sides), a match in which H.V.Dodd brought his record for the season to 100 wickets for 391 runs.

The YMCA also played away matches at the local villages of Slinfold on 13 August, followed by Capel a week later – both matches were won.

Just outside the town of Horsham is the village of Warnham which housed two paternal cricketing powerhouses. The Lucas family lived at Warnham Court and the Harben family at the other end of the village in Warnham Lodge. The 5 September edition of the *West Sussex County Times* told of a match played on Saturday 29 August in which 'There was some interesting cricket at Warnham Lodge.... The village winning before the loss of a single wicket, thanks chiefly to the brilliant batting of C.E.Lucas, who compiled no fewer than 226 before he was stumped.' This was Charles Lucas (Eton and Cambridge) who had played five first-class games for Sussex between 1905 and 1908. The Sussex and future England wicketkeeper, George Street, then 24, was among those playing for Warnham.

And that was it: no further mention of cricket at all. Feelings about playing sport while at war were evidently running high locally as well as nationally, for in the 12 September edition 'A local footballer' wrote to the *West Sussex County Times* saying,

> Football is the working man's sport, so if you propose to stop football, why not stop golf, tennis and other games? They are just as bad or quite as good as football ..... and I think there are others in Horsham who share the same views as myself.

The *Sussex Agricultural Express* for 20 August refers to the cancellation of the rest of the season in the Lewes and District League. The Royal Garrison Artillery at Newhaven had been mobilised and Newhaven (town) had been unable to raise a team either.

The same newspaper (unsurprisingly) comments on the harvest. There was not (yet) a problem with labour, workers not having yet volunteered, though there might be difficulty with laid crops because of the July rains. It argued against the ploughing up of grasslands (but does not suggest a problem with horses).

The edition of 13 August referred to many matches being abandoned because of 'unfavourable weather and the unrest caused by the European War'. This issue did refer to the horse question. Sussex farmers 'have patriotically submitted to the commandeering of their horses for the war' but it was a problem with the harvest to be got in. The government had agreed that where horses were used for agriculture or food distribution, not more than 50% would be taken.

On 6 August again it was reported that Captain Watson (also the captain of Lewes Priory) 'has had to forgo sport for more serious work of a military character'. The paper also carried the 'Your King and Country Need You' advert. Still on that day we have a report of the Southdown Hunt Farmers match. The Master stated that he had placed all his horses at the Kennels at the disposal of the War Office should they need them (applause).

There was still some optimism. Over at St Andrew's, Nuthurst, an ever-hopeful Rev'd J Arthur Rawlins advised parishioners,

> We hope to hold the usual social [in connection with the Dedication Festival] on Thursday Oct 10th, if the war is over by then, otherwise it will not take place this year.

Norfolk seems to have been rather different. The senior clubs played their never-ending round of friendly cricket whilst the village sides' interest was concentrated on the mini-leagues which could be found dotted throughout Norfolk. These competitions, rarely consisting of more than five or six teams, tended to finish as early as mid-July so that they would not be compromised by the harvest; for example, both divisions of the Mid Norfolk Village Shield were settled by 13 July whilst the Honingham & District League was completed just ten days later. Towards the end of the month the rather more urban cup competitions were completed when the final of the Norfolk Junior Cup saw Norwich Stanley crush Yarmouth Southtown by 116 runs and the conclusion of the Junior Cup resulted in Melton Constable thrashing Carrow Seconds by 141 runs.

The press reveals that plenty of midweek matches were played in the last days of July and, further, that a full programme of matches took place on Saturday 1 August. This was reported in the usual manner in the *Eastern Daily Press*: the matches of the senior clubs were dealt with on the following Monday whilst the cards of less important fixtures were printed between Tuesday and Thursday. As was normal, an 'honours board' was also printed which listed those players who had scored at least half a century or taken hauls of five wickets or more; cricketers of all levels of ability were eligible for inclusion and a humble village journeyman could find his name alongside that of a county star.

The Bank Holiday Monday (3 August) also showed a 'normal' pattern for cricket in Norfolk: a number of fixtures of varying importance that one might expect for such a day – Norfolk County Asylum v Lowestoft Town, Overstrand v Carrow, Hunstanton v Stowe & District (who only fielded ten men), Horstead v Old Catton, Somerleyton v Lowestoft Great Eastern Railway, Lexham Park v North Elmham, Dunston v Helpnall, Hasingham v Cantley. It also saw the start of the Festival in which Norfolk hosted Hertfordshire at Lakenham. Fielding a strong eleven, Norfolk took the first-innings points in a game which finished with the visitors needing 39 runs to win with two wickets still to fall.

Although the fact that the Festival had commenced and the fact that results from matches that had been played the previous Saturday were still being reported in the *Eastern Daily Press* rather obscures the picture, it is clear that, while the County side battled on to the end of their programme, both the club and village game came to a complete halt after the 'normal' Bank Holiday. No games at all were played in the next ten days. This was at a time when jingoistic hysteria had yet to dominate the letters column and there was virtually no comment at all in the press at this 'downing of tools'. A note in the *Eastern Daily Press* of 5 August commented matter-of-factly,

> HOLKHAM CRICKET WEEK ABANDONED. Owing to the seriousness of the international situation, the remainder of the matches in the Holkham Cricket Week have been abandoned, and a large bazaar and garden fete, which should have been held in the pleasure grounds in the park in aid of the new Church Rooms at Wells on Thursday has also been postponed. We understand that Oxford Emeriti are abandoning their Norfolk tour.

Other clubs whose visits to Norfolk were cancelled included Merion and the Harlequins. Just two days later another report revealed that sports other than cricket had postponed or cancelled some events: yachting, bowls, lawn tennis, athletics and the following of otter hounds were all listed as being affected. Rather puzzling was the note that there were two remaining matches to be contested in the Earl of Leicester Shield (Warnham had yet to play their return matches with Holkham and the Burnhams) and that 'the outstanding fixtures will be played after harvest': either the sub-editor was a hopeless optimist who thought that the Kaiser would be seen off in days rather than years or it was an item of 'old news', written when war was still only a possibility and only printed when it was out of date.

Turning north to Harrogate, the start of the local cricket for the 1914 season was reported in the *Advertiser* in the edition of 2 May, presumably then as now the Friday publication date. The games in the paper that week appeared to be friendlies. The Yorkshire Council and Nidderdale League and 'ordinary' games began the following week on the basis that their games were first reported on 9 May and the season's fixtures were also published that week. There are weekly match reports, which appear to comprise full scorecards only, from then until they ended on 29 August. G.L.Greaves[40] states that the cricket finished on 18 August. Presumably reported on 22 August, and the final week may not have included a Harrogate CC game.

In Bedfordshire, it was reported at Luton Cricket Club's AGM that after the outbreak of war 'only a few of the remaining matches were played.' The AGM (in December) was adjourned in the hope that things might look brighter a few months on. The secretary thought that several clubs had already given up hope for next year, including Bedford, Dunstable and Hitchin.

Cricket was not, of course, the only English village tradition to suffer: many Morris dancing sides were devastated – four of the EFDSS demonstration

---

40   G.L.Greaves, *Over the Summers Again*, a history of Harrogate CC

team of seven died on the Somme - and the tradition, usually carried on by a small group of people in a village, was in many cases not picked up again afterwards. Like the cases where cricket was lost, it contributed to the slow death of the English village[41].

Cricket in the North was almost entirely league cricket. The *Newcastle Journal* reported on the Durham Senior League, the NW Durham League, the North Durham Senior League, the Tyneside Senior League and the West Tyne League.

Meanwhile the Middlesbrough paper covered the North Yorkshire and South Durham League. On 7 August it reported that 'tomorrow is a critical day in the NY&SD League – Guisborough v Darlington, Redcar v Norton, Saltburn v Bishop Auckland etc.

It also gave fixtures for the East Cleveland League, West Cleveland League, Cleveland Minor League, Stockton League, South Durham Combination and the Middlesbrough Church League.

On 24 August the *Newcastle Journal* reported that the Durham Senior League had met and decided as far as possible to complete the league fixtures.

On the same day the *North East Daily Gazette* carried reports on NY&SD and printed a table after 17 games (one to go). Norton had won the league by this stage despite losing to North Ormesby. A.Goodrick of Darlington took six for 4 (all bowled) against West Hartlepool (Ashley Goodrick was to have a substantial career for Durham after the war). There appears to be nothing in the paper the following week (but it was only a 4-page paper).

On 27 August it was reported that G Company of the 4th battalion of the Yorkshire Regiment had beaten Cockerton Ladies 59 to 40.

On Tuesday 8 September there were still results of games in the West Tyne and Tyneside Senior Leagues and notice of a deciding match in the Northern Wednesday League (Tynemouth v Kimblesworth). On Thursday 10 September we have the table for the East Tyne League (some had games to play) and announcing for Saturday the final of the Durham Senior Cup between Westland (Sunderland) and New Brancepeth. Here at least cricket seems to have run to the end of the season.

The *Sports Argus* was a weekly sporting paper published on Saturdays in Birmingham. On 1 August late news gives information about the war. It was keen about the forthcoming 'derby' between Warwickshire and Worcestershire. It reported Birmingham League games, suburban league games and friendly matches. It reported too on the final of the Aston Schools Trophy, where Gower Street had beaten Canterbury Road. There were league tables, too, from the Birmingham Works League and the Parks Association which ran to eight divisions: not to mention the Kidderminster League, the Prudential League and the Wesleyan League.

The final of the Dudley works knockout was played by Palethorpe's and

---

41   Jo Breeze, *The Morris at War*, Roots 372

Netherton Iron Works at the county ground before a crowd of 1,000.

By the next issue on 8 August (a rest week for the Birmingham League because of works holidays) the paper was discussing the formation of sporting battalions in a lengthy column by 'Argus Junior' headed 'War and Cricket'. On the whole it felt that cricket should continue.

'Skipper' wrote that,

> It is difficult to get one's enthusiasm high enough to write about cricket at such a time as this, but I entirely disagree with the views of some people I have heard lately expressed, that sport should be abolished during the war. This is quite a mistaken idea, as sport acts like a kind of safety-valve, and, in common with the theatre and the music-halls is absolutely necessary to distract the thoughts of the people for a little while from the graver issues at stake.

On 22 August the *Argus* still included all the county scores as well as the leagues. The newspaper regularly offered bats for exceptional performances and noted that 'next Saturday' (29th) was effectively the end of the local season as cricket would give way to football. Football clubs were advertising for players and fixtures, but had not yet started to play.

By 28 August cricket had clearly not stopped in Birmingham. The *Evening Despatch* listed local fixtures in Divisions I and II of the Birmingham League, eight divisions of the Parks League, games in the Wesleyan League and a long list of other matches.

Moving across to Lincolnshire, on 15 August the *Grantham Journal* reported that the Belvoir Hunt Servants had cancelled their remaining matches; nearly half of the Hunt's horses had been requisitioned with 'a consequent reduction of the establishment'. While the Belvoir Hunt was more vulnerable than most, horses were frequently need to travel to matches, and both they and motor vehicles were requisitioned very early on.

In Cowbridge, nine members of the club's 1st XI , including their professional, who a month before had enjoyed a jolly tour in North Somerset, all enlisted and soon afterwards made their way to Neyland for military training.

Would requisitioning horses have created a transport problem for local cricket? At the beginning of the war the Army had 25,000 horses (and only 80 motor vehicles) and requisitioned another 165,000 horses over the first two weeks: the Army was looking for 500,000. And what were the rules? Farming in 1914 surely could not have operated without horses to pull the ploughs and the farm carts – oxen had mostly disappeared and motor vehicles were far and few between. They certainly could not have been spared to move village cricket teams around.

It was not quite the end of the season, but there was a peculiar incident on 25 August at Tonbridge. Kent Club & Ground had set the touring Merion Cricket Club (from Philadelphia) to make 153 in 55 minutes. With two balls to go they needed two to win with seven wickets left. G.J.V.Weigall (who Allen Synge called 'a laughing cavalier of cricket'), captaining the Kent side, ordered the last two balls to be rolled along the ground to prevent their being hit and the match was drawn. This a friendly match! What the Philadelphians had done to warrant this passes all understanding. It was the last match of the tour and an extraordinary finale.

Chapter Ten

Will There Be Cricket in 1915?

The question now passed to other sports and it becomes clear that (for whatever reason) there was a split along class lines. Professional football – the Football League, the Southern League, the Birmingham Combination – continued for 1914/15. The amateur leagues (Isthmian and Athenian) did not. All the rugby union clubs in the South and Midlands stopped, but for 1914/15 Rugby Union continued in Wales, where it was a working-class game: the Northern Union (Rugby League) continued.

Rugby Union in England in 1914 was very much a gentleman's game. The insistence on the most punctilious amateurism and the fact that only public schools played the game ensured that this was the officer class, and many of them would have been recalled to their regiments right at the start – which would have taken organisers as well as players.

It was agreed in February 1915 that the Lancashire League would go on as usual though with reduced wages for professionals and allowances would be discontinued for amateurs. Mr Barlow (Secretary) said, 'if it had not been for that madman the Kaiser, he would have to report the most successful season ever experienced.' There would be no junior 2nd XI championship in 1915, though.

Most famously, the Bradford League played on right through the war, attracting many professionals whose wartime occupations allowed. The full story is told in *Cricket's Wartime Sanctuary* by Tony Barker[42] .

Other matches for 1915 on *CricketArchive* are all school games with a couple of military games at the start of the year.

According to the *Yorkshire Evening Post* in April 2015,

> The Yorkshire Cricket Council and most of the important cricket leagues of Yorkshire have entirely suspended competitive sport for the coming season, arrangements are being made in many quarters for carrying on the game purely as a recreation and relaxation from the serious business of the day.

it then gives a long list of Yorkshire Council and Leeds League clubs who have arranged friendly fixtures.

In May 1915 Kent had arranged friendlies with Surrey and Yorkshire 'if the war is over soon enough'. It wasn't.

Minor leagues in Yorkshire continued – the *Yorkshire Evening Post* covers

---

42   Tony Barker, *Cricket's Wartime Sanctuary*, ACS Publications, 2009

scores from the Airedale and Wharfedale League, the Leeds Sunday Schools League, Bradford League, Huddersfield and District League, the Spen Valley and District League with Yorkshire Council and Leeds League clubs playing friendlies. There is still a long list of scores in September.

The Ribblesdale League did not continue long: in fact it packed up early in August 1914.

In May 1916 Broad Oak was reported to have withdrawn from the Huddersfield Central League as 19 out of 26 regulars had joined up. On 25 May 1916 the *Yorkshire Post* published a Huddersfield and District League table.

The Halifax League played. The Halifax Parish Cricket League actually started (as an adjustment of existing leagues) in 1914 with ten clubs (all village sides). They played (with only seven clubs) in 1915 and 1916.

Again in 1916 the Lancashire League continued (with amateurs only). Other matches on *CricketArchive* are school games.

The Lancashire League was much restricted in 1917 – according to David Edmundson[43] the clubs agreed in February to abandon the season and the same was true in 1918 though a knockout competition was played.

The Central Lancashire League shows champions all through the war.

So it is hard to discern overall patterns: yes, the north was more likely to play on than the south, the working classes than the middle classes. Perhaps though those who played on were the ones who saw cricket as just a recreation or an entertainment rather than a kind of magic ritual of Englishness. Or it may have been that the upper and upper-middle classes volunteered or were recalled to their regiments while many working-class cricketers were needed to carry on in the mines and factories.

Cricket was never the same after the war: and yet it was, and Eric Midwinter has argued that a longing for things to be as they had been ossified a game that needed to change to maintain its appeal.

---

43   David Edmundson, *See The Conquering Hero, the story of the Lancashire League*, Mike McLeod Litho, 1992

Thanks to Contributors

Though my name is on the cover, this book is in essence a collaboration between a number of ACS members, and I am deeply grateful to all of them.

The original idea was Roger Moulton's and he left me to run with it as I pleased. There was also important support from John Bryant. Professor Eric Midwinter kindly wrote a piece which is now the foreword of the book.

Other contributors who researched what had happened in their own localities (and here in no particular order) included Stephen Musk (Norfolk), David Main (Scotland), Jack Gillett (Kent), Stephen Baldwin (Leamington), David Pracy (Essex), Dave Boorman (Sussex), Chris Overson (Harrow), Keith Walmsley (Berkshire), Julian Lawton Smith (Oxfordshire), Andrew Hignell (Wales), Mick Pope and Mark Rowe.

I am also grateful to the Lord's library for the chance to read *World of Cricket* and to Phil Hadwen for the loan of a number of county histories.

I should also like to thank Roger Moulton for his work as editor, Ric Finlay and John Ward for proofreading and Jenny Moulton for compiling the index.

I am most grateful to the following who provided pictures: David Griffin (Derbyshire), Andrew Hignell (Neath CC), Roger Gibbons (Gloucestershire), Dave Allen (Hampshire), David Robertson (Kent), Richard Holdridge (Leicestershire), John Watson Northamptonshire), Peter Wynne-Thomas (Nottinghamshire), Steve Hill (Somerset), Bill Gordon (Surrey), Sussex Cricket Museum (Sussex), Phil Britt (Warwickshire), Tim Jones (Worcestershire), Mick Pope and Brian Sanderson (Yorkshire), Tim Jones for producing the Essex/Worcestershire photograph and David Pracy for his help in identifying the Essex players, Mary-Louise Rowland (Hurstpierpoint College), Alexandra Aslett (St Paul's School) and Tom Moulton (St Lawrence College).

I must also thank Emily Sweetman for designing the cover and also all those at City Press involved in typesetting and printing.

Bibliography

Among the books consulted on general history:

AJP Taylor, *English History 1914-1945,* Oxford UP, 1965
IF Clarke (ed.), *Voices Prophesying War 1763-1984,* Panther Arts, 1970
Barbara W Tuchman, *The Guns of August,* Ballantine, 1994
Adrian Gregory, *The Last Great War,* Cambridge UP, 2008
Robert Roberts, *The Classic Slum,* Penguin
Bertrand Russell, *Autobiography*
Sean McMeek, *July 1914, Countdown to War,* 2014
Christopher Clarke, *The Sleepwalkers,* Penguin, 2013
Robert Graves, *Goodbye To All That,* Penguin ,1960
Nigel Fountain (edit), *When The Lamps Went Out,* 2014
Malcolm Brown, *1914 The Men Who Went To War,* Imperial War Museum, 2014

And on cricket:

First-Class Cricket Matches 1914, ACS Publications, 2008
Andrew Searle, *SF Barnes, His Life and Times,* Empire Publications, 1997
Philip Bailey, Philip Thorn, Peter Wynne-Thomas, *Who's Who of Cricketers,*
    Guild Publishing, 1984
Leslie Duckworth: *SF Barnes, Master Bowler,* Cricketer/Hutchinson, 1967
Leo McKinstry: *Jack Hobbs, England's Greatest Cricketer,* Yellow Jersey, 2012
James P Coldham , *Lord Hawke, a cricketing legend,* Tauris Park Paperbacks, 2003
Ric Sissons,*The Players,* Kingswood, 1988
Gerard Siggins, *Green Days: Cricket in Ireland 1792-2005,* Nonsuch, 2005
HW Lee, *Forty Years of English Cricket,* Clerke & Cockeran, 1948
AW Ledbrooke, *Lancashire County Cricket – the official history 1864-1953,*
    Phoenix House, 1954
FS Ashley-Cooper, *Middlesex County Cricket Club 1900-1920,*
    William Heinemann, 1921
Peter Wynne-Thomas, *Trent Bridge,* Notts County Council, 1987
GW Egdell and MFK Fraser, *Warwickshire County Cricket Club: a history,*
    Cornish Bros, 1946
Robert Brooke, *F.R.Foster The Fields Were Sudden Bare,* ACS Publications, 2012
Alan West : *100 years of the Ribblesdale League,* Preston, 1992
Roy Genders, *Worcestershire,* Convoy Publications, 1952
Allen Synge, *Sins of Omission,* Pelham Books, 1990
Neville Cardus, *English Cricket,* Collins, 1945
Andrew Renshaw (edit), *Wisden on the Great War,* Bloomsbury, 2014
Peter Davies and David Normanton, *100 Years of Hilltop and Valley-Bottom Cricket*
    (History of the Halifax Cricket League), 2014
David W Potter, *The Encyclopaedia of Scottish Cricket,* 1999
Peter Wynne-Thomas, *Cricket's Historians,* ACS Publications, 2011
Giles Phillips : *On Fenner's Sward,* Tempus, 2005
Jack Chapman : *Cream Teas and Nutty Slack,* self, 2012
JB Hobbs : *My Cricket Memories,* Heinemann, 1924
Bernard Harrison and Phil Bichard, *Basingstoke & North Hants Cricket Club*
    1865-1965, self published, 1965
Tony Barker, *Cricket's Wartime Sanctuary,* ACS, 2009

Newspapers etc

The Times, Manchester Guardian, Daily Mirror, Daily Express.
World of Cricket.

Index

This index is very largely restricted to cricketers, clubs and schools.